Index to Ethical Theory: An Antholog
Copyright © James Lane, 2022

First published 2022

James Lane
ISBN 9798484095308

The author is thankful for the kind permission of Russ
Shafer-Landau and Wiley-Blackwell publishers to compile this
index. They assert the following rights concerning the work on
which this index is based (as italicized):

Deepest gratitude to Alforus, West Heidelberg, for all your help.

Thanks also go to Hesham Gneady and the team at PDF Index
Generator (pdfindexgenerator.com).

In loving memory of Joc Forsyth
stakkels mand, far far, bull ant man, salmonella seeker
(1930 – 2022)

Index to Ethical Theory: An Anthology

Symbols

2+2=4 (or 5), 175, 245

A

a fortiori:. *See also a priori*
actions, 163, 529
interests, 374
moral outlook, 90
rights, 385
a priori:
agent neutrality, 150
argument, 55
categorical imperative, 492, 494
causal theories, 794
conditions/ relations, 13
contingency, 787
discipline, 55
intuition, 104
intuitive reactions, 83
justification, 109
law, 230, 495
logical question, 97
optimific act, 760
philosophy, 54–55, 495
prima facie duty, 758
proposition, 106, 109, 492
psychology, 318
purpose, 490
reasoning, 786
statements, 174, 177

theorem, 103
truth, 174, 223
utilitarianism, 463
abduction, 112
Abelard, Peter, 178, 190, 654
Dialogue between a Philosopher, a Jew, and a Christian, 178
abortion:. *See also baby/babies*
Abortion and Infanticide (chapter 46, Tooley, Michael), 390–399
abortion study, the, 697–698
Argument that Abortion is Wrong, An (chapter 47, Marquis, Don), 400–409
caring, ethic of, and, 703–704
dilemma of choice, and, 695
disagreement over, 96, 369
future value of fetuses, and, 357
killing and letting die, and, 551
male inapplicability, 362
partial-birth, 91

personhood (i.e. properties of a person), and, 390
Problem of Abortion and the Doctrine of the Double Effect, The (chapter 60, Foot, Philippa), 399, 536–542
recent discussion of, 39
right to, 361
three moral perspectives, and, 695
Virtue Theory and, 675
Virtue Theory and Abortion (Hursthouse, Rosalind), 664, 675
Abraham (Luke 16:24-26), 709
absolution, 136, 315, 471
absolutism, 18, 437, 477, 707, 754, 768
accomplishment, 199, 204, 638
account/s:
developmental, 681
introspective, 794
Achilles, 99, 415
acorns, 135
action/s (Handlung):
abstain from, 700
cause of, 376

1

ground floor reason
for, 179
guiding, 25, 30, 109,
647–648, 737,
741–742
human, 64, 142, 167,
223, 246, 261,
299, 310, 317–318,
417, 496, 513,
566, 655–657
interpersonal, 524
overriding reason for,
107
prospective, 107
right and good, 666
rightness of, 17, 423,
533, 664, 672
theory of, 550
actions and ends, 491
activism, 518, 520, 733
Adams, Robert
Merrihew, 216–224,
247–252, 275–276
New Divine Command
Theory, A (chapter
24), 220–224
reasons of gratitude,
247
Addelson, Kathryn,
738, 749
adducing
considerations, 116
Adeimantus (elder
half-brother of
Plato), 135, 572.
See also Glaucon
(elder half-brother
of Plato)
adolescence, 32, 650,
692–693, 696, 698,
723
adult/s:
ethics, 696

femininity and
adulthood, 695
love, 344, 696
moral conception, 698
normal, 105, 368–369,
372
work, 696, 698
adultery, 625, 757
Aeschylus, 134
Harvesting a deep
furrow in his mind,
134
aesthete, pure, 203
aesthetics/ æsthetics:
enjoyment, 302, 403
evaluative analogue,
327
happiness, 171
innovative, 181
judgments, 30
moral considerations,
vs, 236
pleasure, 172, 296
reasons, 92, 235
speculative knowledge,
as, 16
statements, 16
values, 22, 30
affection:
actions of others, and,
342
affectional grounds, 92
arbitrary, 215
Chisholm, for, 268
complaisance, 567
disaffection, 204
entitlement to, 94
good will, 207
interdependence, 736
intimates, and,
441–446
moral constraint, 572
moral/ity, 10, 572, 580
plants, for, 375

pleasure, 256
reactive attitude, 307
reason and, 10
undeserving of, 290
unreasonable, 8
Africa, 539, 703
agency:
causation and, 81
genuine, 327
intentional, 332
purposive, 534
agent (agere):
acts and, 36–38, 60,
147, 239, 309–311,
333, 338, 342,
344, 419, 422,
431, 435, 438–439,
445, 449, 451,
456–457, 506
aims/ interests/
purposes of, 149,
152, 156–157,
161–162, 183,
234–238, 343,
504, 507–511
autonomous, 519
based, 653–663
crimes by, 327
deep selves of,
332–333
desires of, 24, 130,
139–140, 144–145,
148, 152, 159–160,
165, 184, 332–333,
349, 504, 507,
524–526. *See also*
desire/s (Begier)
duties and, 60, 526
effects on, 185, 188,
234
efforts of, 520
existence of, 306
factors beyond control
of, 325, 327, 332,

343, 383
fallibility and, 56
free/dom of, 238, 318,
320, 331, 348
future self of, 155
happiness of, 417
harm to, 512
idealized human, as,
54
in/sanity of, 335, 338,
344, 346. *See also*
Catch-22
judged, 37, 160–161,
422, 452
judgment by, 325
justification of, 57,
147, 161, 238,
306, 309, 383
knowledge of, 20
moral choices and, 63,
120
moral judgments and,
30, 435, 792
motive of, 20, 67,
160, 169–170,
176, 383, 386–387,
418
neutral, 144, 148,
150–152, 156–157
patient and, 381
person vs, 394
perspective of,
164–165, 185, 209
pleasure of, 300
predilections of, 534
promises and, 501
prospective, 529
prospective purposive,
531–532
qua recipient,
524–525, 528,
531, 533
qualified, 664–666,
673

reasons for action by,
37, 66, 130, 144,
147–148, 150–160,
188, 235
reasons for beliefs,
164, 790–791
regret, 324, 328
relative, 144–148,
150, 152–157, 188
responsibility and,
330–335, 338,
343, 421
rights of, 483
self-interest of, 179,
183, 420
supernatural, 59
unique entity, as, 306,
483
values of, 190
virtuous, 157,
646–649, 651–652,
655, 664–666,
670, 673–674
well-being of, 178, 514
wrongdoing by, 159,
345, 392, 433
aggregative, 604
agreeing to differ/
disagree, 98
agreement:
hypothetical, 577–579,
582, 597
informed, 597
mediated, 694
relevant, 583
unanimous, 575, 603,
605
aid:
Bengal, to, 466
bringing, 540–541
mutual, 39, 146–147,
149, 506, 598
positive aid, 540
airheads, 684

Albritton, Rogers, 143
Alfred, Alfrieda,
Charles, David,
Edward, Frank,
George, Harry,
Irving (fictitious
characters),
543–551
algebraic sum of
advantages, 582
algorithm, 125, 612,
631, 788
alien, 98, 441, 453–454,
456, 640, 705
alienation, 446–450
all things equal,
781–782, 789
alms, giving, 757, 769
for the praise of men,
141
altruism:
absolute, 525
deceptive, 171
devoting energy
towards, 206
egoism and, 707
egotism vs, 21
ethics of, 195–196
impartial, 433
inner strength, 659
moral praise, and, 207
morally important act,
323
positive moral
interests, 207
Possibility of Altruism,
The (Nagel,
Thomas), 151, 158
Rand, Ayn, on,
195–196
repayment, 658
sacrifice and, 151
societal contentment,
21

INDEX TO ETHICAL THEORY: AN ANTHOLOGY

Ambrosius, 470
amenability, 309
**Amy, Jake, Ned, Diane
    & Sharon
    (research
    respondents),**
    692–698
anaesthetic, 95–96
analogue, 120, 327,
    346–348, 408, 594,
    660–661, 677
    evaluative, 327
analogy:
    abortion - animals, 406
    agent- neutrality
        (Kant), 151
    argument from, 163,
        793
    arts - virtues, 666
    builder - morality,
        681, 685
    color blindness, 81
    decision theory, 125
    disanalogy, 75, 82,
        163–164, 635
    dominance and, 202
    empirical observation,
        75–80, 84
    freedom of action, 331
    happiness maximizing
        and other ends,
        446
    Health-Pebble, 547
    human service, 359
    infants - fetuses, 402
    intuitions, 108
    meaning in lives -
        meaning in
        language, 455
    moral - logical -
        mathematical
        (Ross), 108
    moral theory -
        scientific theory,

743
    morality - etiquette
        (Foot), 149
    narration, deduction,
        and, 745
    narrative, and, 745
    prior cases, from,
        792–793
    rational choice (utility
        theory), 120
    self-love, fear,
        inclination, 497
    speciesism, 356, 363
    two principles of
        justice - maximin
        rule (choice under
        uncertainty),
        589–591
    utilitarianism,
        consequentialism,
        over-demandingness
        criticism, 660
    Vindication of the
        Rights of Brutes, A
        (Taylor, Thomas),
        361
analysis:
    conceptual, 26, 28,
        223, 382, 529–531,
        734
    cost-benefit, 432, 434,
        438
    logical, 40, 378
    psychoanalysis, 642
Ancient Rome, 44
anger, 136, 318, 344,
    366–367, 373, 562,
    634–635, 701
animal/s:
    actions and, 332–333
    acts of, 359
    appetites, 258
    beasts of burden, 41,
        629

beasts, as, 97,
    258–259, 563–564,
    633, 732
behaviour of, 292, 308
benefitting from, 357
benevolence and, 170
Benevolent Protective
    Order of Elks, 163
bird (defining), 790
cat, 5, 32–34, 359,
    361, 374, 377,
    393, 397, 706
catfish, 781
cerebral cortex of, 366
chimera/ chimaera, 9,
    49
chimpanzee, 367,
    369–370
communication, 367
confining animals to
    machines, 292
de nuce, asino et
    muliere, 360
diencephalon of, 366
different to human
    beings, 368, 573
dog, 35, 106, 115,
    177, 267, 279,
    359–362, 364–365,
    369–370, 374,
    377, 382, 573, 672
domestic, 97
duties towards (or lack
    of), 359–360
eating animals, 779
elephant, 375
equality and, 364
experiences of, 265
experimentation on,
    357, 359–360, 368
farm, 355
good of, the, 291–292
guppies, 357
horse, 48–49, 51–52,

4

INDEX TO ETHICAL THEORY: AN ANTHOLOGY

98, 133, 168, 319,
361, 364, 368,
464–465, 615,
618–620, 624
husbandry, 357
incest among, 14
individual, 372, 375
Kant on, 355–356,
359–360
killing, 368–369
kingdom, 701
kittens (torturing), 678
lamb, 135
laughing, 642
liberation, 361–362
limited understanding
of, 368
lion, 173, 228
love and, 291
lower, 228, 259, 332
moral concern for, 370
moral standing and,
356
self- consciousness
requirement,
390, 398
mouse, 364, 369
nature, 87, 260, 292,
359, 636, 733
nervous system of, 366
nonhuman, 87,
355–357, 361,
365–369, 703
opossum, 669–670
pain and, 291, 300,
366–369
pigs, 170, 256,
258–259, 272,
327, 363, 369–370,
703
pleasure of, 300–301
rat, 772
rational, 395

responsibility and,
309–311, 332–333
rights of, 361, 364,
372–373, 375,
377, 379, 386, 389
sacrificial, 195
self-moving, 311
sentience of, 300
sheep, 133, 135
slaves, comparison
with, 364
sparrow, 319
speciesism, 365,
368–371
studies on, 367
suffering, 364, 367
swallow, 618
swan, 175
tortoise, 99
vivisection and, 359
wild, 368
animism, 321
Annas, Julia, 613–614,
779, 783–784
Being Virtuous and
Doing the Right
Thing (chapter 71),
676–686
**Anscombe, Gertrude
Elizabeth Margaret,**
30, 143, 542
**ant and the
grasshopper, the,**
787
antebellum mansion,
277–278
anthropology, 27,
44–45, 351, 427,
459, 572, 640–641,
674
antirealism, 55–57,
59–62
antitheory, 650–651,
738, 776–777

anxiety, 340, 367, 442,
488–489, 491, 739
anything goes, 246,
640, 774
appeal to:
authority, 227, 475
consistency, 787
custom, 475
intuition, 18
moral authority, 788
obviousness, 101
principle, 677
procedure, 788
virtues (the), 239, 788
appeal, surreptitious,
116
**appearance and
reality,** 98
appetite/s (cupiditas):
animal, 14, 258, 374
base, 628
bodily, 632–634, 636
conditioned responses,
331
contractors, 567
discourse, 637
good and evil, 569
good, to, 9
Greek thought, and,
636
meat, for, 636
object of, 636
pathetic fallacy, 30
rational will (voluntas),
vs, 528
reason, 622
sexual, 636
virtue, 624, 637
apprehension:
apprehending truth/
self-evidence,
102–103
beauties and defects,
of, 759

dangers, of, 492
fallible, 227
feminine, 695
meaning/s of, 759
modes of, 696
moral principles, of, 709–710
moral realm, of the, 227
objective truths, of, 27
physical world, of the, 227
prima facie rightness/ wrongness, of, 759–761
Aquinas, Thomas, 470, 473, 528, 535, 725
arbitrariness, 215, 475, 477, 527, 578, 638, 754
arbitrary arrest, 586
arbitrary restrictions, 406
arbitrator, 567–569
Archilochus, 136–137
fox and the hedgehog, the, 137
aretaic, 653–654, 656–657, 659
Argentina, 323
argument:
analogical, 163–164, 166
analogous, 95, 98, 793
basic, 312–316, 390
disagreement, from, 56, 97–98
presumptive, 78, 160
queerness, from, 26, 28–29
relativity, from, 27
theoretical, 137
vicious circle, 71, 73

aristotelian:
concepts, 30
moral philosophy, 207
neo- Aristotelian, 157, 647, 663
non- Aristotelian, 30
Non-relative virtues, 630–644
Non-Relative Virtues: An Aristotelian Approach (chapter 67, Nussbaum, Martha), 630–644
Proceedings of the Aristotelian Society (citations), 275–276, 322, 328, 685, 794
reasons for action, 38
right actions, notion of , 792
strategy, 153
tradition, 67
virtue ethicist, 612
virtuous agent, 665
Aristotle:
affiliation, 642
agency, on, 310–311
cognitive capability, on , 641
common humanity, features of, 641
equality, on, 578
friendship, on, 153, 191
guilt cultures, on, 313
happiness, on, 268
human good, on, 642–643
humor, 642
infants, on, 378
megalopsuchia (μεγαλοψυχια), 635

Nature of Virtue, The (chapter 66), 615–629
Nichomachean Ethics, 615
Non-Relative Virtues: An Aristotelian Approach (chapter 67, Nussbaum, Martha), 630–644
pleasures, on, 271–272
self-fulfilment, on, 173
virtue, on, 615–631
around here, 680
arrested development, 679
arrogance, 160, 485, 569, 666, 674, 745
art:
appeal of, 171
art lovers, 374
artist/s, 171, 202, 278, 324
competition, 134
connoisseurship, 668
dislike of, 171
foundations, 668
happiness and, 171
high-end, 755
moral views and, 779
Museum of Modern Art , 779
navigation as an, 421, 425
performance, 681
pleasure in, 274
practical, 421
profession, 7
sculpture, 618
statues, 134
Taj Mahal as, 374
technical, 491
terms of, 562
theft of, 274

valuable items, 668
artifact, 59, 81, 149,
 732, 748, 790
 ornamental, 374
aseity, 315
aspire to improve, 682
assault, 731
Astaire, Fred, 206
asymmetry, 793
atheism, 216–217, 220,
 225–229, 245, 314,
 571
atomism, 772–774
attitude/s:
 expression of, 25
 intentions and, 343
 moral, 20, 29–30,
  326–328, 348–349,
  351, 469
 objective, 344–352
 pro-attitude, 84, 145,
  150, 152, 427
 reactive, 307,
  343–350, 742
 shared, 40
Audi, Robert, 6, 72,
 667, 669, 675, 768,
 771
 Moral Knowledge and
  Ethical Pluralism
  (chapter 13),
  101–111
Augustine of Hippo,
 Saint (Aurelius
 Augustinus
 Hipponensis), 528,
 535, 654
austere moralist, 299
authenticity, 446
authority, 495, 539,
 677, 691, 731,
 735–750
 absolute, 30
 appeal to, 227, 475

authority, objective, 5,
 30
 distribution of,
  583–586
 ethics, of, 25
 external/ independent,
  26, 421
 independence from,
  693
 intellect, of, 726
 legitimate, 670
 moral judgments, of,
  85–89
 moral law, of, 143, 157
 morality, of, 144–159
 parental, 723
 rules, of, 3
 sovereign, 560
 special, 149–150
 state, 555
autonomy:
 ability and, 693
 compassion and, 695
 damage to, 515, 519
 detachment and, 724
 emergent, 693
 goal, as a, 446–448,
  515–516
 growth/ development
  and, 698, 722
 human quality, as a,
  288–289, 355–356,
  429, 482
 importance of,
  161–163, 723, 727
 justice and, 714
 limited, 513–514, 723
 moral interdependency
  and, 716
 moral tradition and,
  724
 partial, 517
 preoccupation with,
  736

reason, of, 232
respect for, 648–649,
 665, 723
will, of the, 233
women and, 725, 748
avalanche, 228, 295,
 548
aversion, 4, 7–9, 64,
 262, 279, 291, 488,
 567, 569, 587
Ayer, Alfred Jules
 "Freddie", 4–6,
 306, 705
 Critique of Ethics, A
  (chapter 2), 16–21
 Freedom and
  Necessity (chapter
  38), 317–321

B

baby/babies:. _See also_
 abortion;
 child/ren,
 childhood
 abortion, 39, 91, 96,
  357–358, 361–362,
  369, 390–395,
  397–403, 405–409,
  536–539, 541–543,
  551, 664, 675,
  695, 697–698,
  703–704, 727. _See_
  also baby/babies;
  infanticide
 bathing, 65, 325
 drowning, 65, 325
 killing, 44, 390–399,
  402, 502, 551, 704
 life stage, 32
 newborn, 378, 398,
  502
 parental desire, 289

slapping, 368
torture, 245, 773
backsliding, 775
bad government, 765
bad woman, 695
Baier, Annette, 690,
719–720, 777, 784
Need for More than
Justice, The
(chapter 75),
721–728
Baier, Kurt E. M.,
197–198, 535
Bambrough, Renford,
6, 72
Proof (chapter 12),
94–100
bargaining, 39–40,
512, 514, 578, 589,
597, 736
Baron, Marcia, 717
basing requirement,
122, 126
bathing, 172
beauty:
awareness of true
beauty, 296–298
better world and, 256
biotic community, 381
conceit, 326
happiness, 620
hedonism, 297
intrinsic value, 255,
448
Large City, 548
limitation and, 643
maximizing, 413
moral, 13
moral duty, 753
nonutilitarians and,
205
Objective List Theory,
296
plants, 375

values and, 22
virtue, 668
Beauvoir, Simone de,
689
because, 29, 789
because they are right,
141, 216
bedrock, 637, 640, 642
begging priests, 135
begging the question,
57–58, 87, 164, 204,
234, 238, 245, 310,
357, 402, 450, 476,
732, 767, 774
beginning of our lives,
the, 760
being rather than
doing, 648
being told what to do,
678–679
belief/s:
background, 220
conflicting, 58, 638
evaluative, 113
explanatory, 718
false, 6, 23, 65, 67,
71, 90, 277,
281–283, 336,
338, 597, 674
forming, 87, 124
inferentially justified,
101
justifiable, 121–123
justified, 55, 57–58,
61–62, 73, 101,
103, 105, 109–110,
114–117, 119,
124, 755
non-inferentially
justified, 101
nonevaluative, 113
noninferred, 122
other, 115
privileging, 121

set of, 118–120, 122,
124–125
spontaneous, 121
transfers, 531
believing vs doing, 120
beneficence
(Wohltätigkeit,
Wohltun):
duty/ies and, 102,
515, 757, 763–764,
766–769
egoism and, 195
non-maleficence vs,
757
benevolence
(Wohlwollen):
alleviating need, 669
animals and, 170
caring, 656
choice situation,
606–607
compassion, kindness,
and, 659
consequentialism, 690
desires, 9
disinterested, 169–170
duty, 757, 769
exhibiting, 655
gratitude, 567
impersonal, 690
Kant, 206–207
knee-jerk actions, 669
morality as, 662–663
motivation, 422,
655–656
ought-judgments, 40
pleasure, 170
promise-keeping and,
757, 769
respect, 233
universal, 659–661
universal law, 494
utilitarian, 427, 482
virtue, 665, 668, 670

benevolent impulses, 582
Bengal Relief Fund, 469
Benhabib, Seyla, 715–716
Bentham, Jeremy (Benthamian, Benthamites), 167–168, 171, 255–256, 356, 363–364, 367, 413, 422–423, 428, 536
Bernard J. Ortcutt (fictitious character), 36–38
best self, 315, 700
beyond the pale, 37
bias, 107, 363, 427, 601, 690, 713–715, 718–719, 722, 736, 739–740, 749
biblical literalism, 223
bilateral exchange, 522
bindingness, 761
biological propensities, 386
biotic community, 381, 387
birth control, 96, 695
black holes, 34
blades of grass, 296–297
blank slate, 677
bliss, 264–265, 314
blood, 32, 366, 401, 544, 695, 774
blood transfusion, 774
bloodless, 193
Blum, Lawrence, 722
boat, in the same, 63, 166, 749
bombs, 168, 272, 379,

396, 424, 545–546, 548–550
boredom, 19
Bradley, Francis Herbert, 152, 157
brain damage, 369, 377
brain in a vat, 86, 90, 270, 782
brain-washing, 57, 225, 331–334
Branden, Barbara, 196
Brandt, Richard B., 271, 275–277, 279, 285
bravery, 23, 418, 616, 620, 622–623, 625–628, 676, 682–683
Brentano, Franz Clemens, 272–276
intentional states, 155
Bricker, P., 298
Brink, David O., 130
Puzzle About the Rational Authority of Morality, A (chapter 17), 144–158
Brouwer, Luitzen Egbertus Jan (Bertus), 594, 596
builder, 567, 614, 622, 681–682, 684
busybodying, 679

C

cabin boy, 541
Cairns, Huntington, 158
cake:
ginger, 99

have our cake and eat it, 61, 226, 690
calculation:
ideal calculator of consequences, 683
probabilistic calculations, 590
utilitarian, 107, 204, 426
Calhoun, Cheshire, 690, 738, 749
Justice, Care, and Gender Bias (chapter 74), 713–720
Cambridge- change, 295
Canada, 676
cancer research, 536, 538
canon, 494, 529–531, 716
capital punishment (death penalty), 96, 404, 675, 710–711
capitalism, 720, 779
caprice/ capricious, 310–311, 519, 793
captain, 134
care:
ability to, 708
activity of, 696, 723
aged, for the, 97
animals and, 279, 369, 374
avoidance of, 704
buzzword, as a, 721
care ethics, 690, 713–714, 719, 721, 726
cared-for, 700–710
categorical imperative and, 142, 455

charity and, 194, 703
circles of caring, 704
concern and, 695
duty and, 717
ethical caring, 699,
704, 707
ethics of, 690,
695–696, 698,
703, 709, 713–714,
719, 724, 726
etiquette and, 139
everyone, for, 702
examining arguments
with, 141
fairness and, 698
feminine goodness and
, 696
fetuses and, 402
givers, 737
god/s, of/by, 134, 240
greed and, 338
health/ medical,
466–468, 518–519,
745
human vegetables and
, 377
ideal of, 724
injunction to, 697
intimacy and, 737
life and, 455
love and, 289
moral requirements
and, 5
morality and, 241,
431, 594
mutual, 723
natural caring (or
caring naturally),
699–704, 707
needy (the) and, 656
obligation and, 700,
702
one-caring, 700–711
other-selves, for, 153

others and, 142, 145,
199–200, 416,
433, 455, 483,
494, 548, 557,
572, 598, 640,
660, 690, 695,
701, 707
parental/ children and,
171, 348, 359,
369, 402, 446,
532, 542, 695–696,
699, 701, 725, 727
perspective, 722
pleasure and, 428
preservation of life and
, 487
qualities and, 290
reflective
understanding of,
698
remote descendents
and, 372
research/ discussion/
assessment and,
50, 179, 582, 585,
633, 763
responsibility and,
330, 695, 697–698,
724
self-, 196, 557, 565,
657, 701, 710, 727
sick, for the, 205
specific people, for,
92, 442, 448, 576,
727, 736
taker, 710
taking, 446, 657,
696–697, 701, 723
things and, 290–291,
374
thoughtfulness and,
511
understanding and,
628, 723

winning and, 445
women and, 697
Carroll, Lewis, 99
Carson, Thomas, 257
Rationality and Full
Information
(chapter 32),
277–285
cart before the horse,
98
case/s:
arguing from the, 539
being under the
impression that
so-and-so is the
case, 301
borderline, 373, 745
case by case, 150,
293, 774, 779
case-specific (moral)
intuitions, 72–75,
78–84
class of, 376
comparing, 107
hard, 403, 572
hypothetical, 59, 107,
238
imaginary, 83, 462
just in case, 3, 66,
148–149, 153,
247, 255, 306,
613, 753
kinds of, 83, 186, 237,
246, 290, 426–427,
460, 501, 508,
539, 548, 747,
755, 760, 782
limiting, 42
particular cases, 32,
41, 74–75, 82,
108, 345–347,
350, 424–425,
435, 446, 585,
623, 625–626,

649, 715, 737,
742–743, 755,
767, 785, 787
principle subsuming a
case, 106
sufficient similarity,
96, 599, 792–793
two, 34, 186, 324,
329, 396, 519,
545, 758–759,
766, 787–788, 793
what is the case, 4, 96
casual influence, 759
casuistry, 21, 421, 785
catch red-handed, 133
Catch-22, 338
Catholic, 223, 536–537,
541–542
caught, getting/being,
36, 236
cause (cf Ursache)
   causality:
aseity, 315
causal connection, 24,
27, 336, 505,
515–516, 518
causal contact, 34
causal efficacy (or
inefficacy), 55, 59,
62, 277, 332
causal law/s, 310,
317, 321, 509
causal role, 222
causal test, 59–62
causation and agency,
81
cause and effect, 8,
13, 352
cause of action, 376
self-caused (causa sui)
, 312, 315
certain (crucial)
   mental respects,
312, 314–315

ceteris paribus,
781–782, 789
chain of facts, 701
Chamberlain, Neville,
325
character traits:
acting rightly, 451
excellence, 204
judgment, 785
Kantian saint, 206
moral good, 208
utilitarian saint, 206
virtues/ vices, 207,
611, 647, 652–653,
676
characterizable, 123
charity:
acts of, 469, 540–541
Amnesty International,
226, 229
degrading, 194–195
donating/ giving to,
86, 437, 469
duty and, 469–470,
515, 540–541
hypothetical
imperative, 142
justice vs, 649
optional, 726
Oxfam, 201, 203, 314,
439, 452
reasons for, 216
reputation of, 142, 561
rights-based thinking,
vs, 519
rule of, 142
virtue, 142, 648, 650
cheating, 421, 505,
508, 513, 555
checklist:
artificialities, 104
theory, 790

**Chesterton, Gilbert
Keith,** 176
Father Brown, 202
St Francis of Assisi,
202
child/ren, childhood:.
*See also
baby/babies*
accidental killing of,
324–325
anaesthetic and, 95–96
child abuse, 226
desire theory and, 289
great- grandchildren,
379
happy, 171, 274, 294
innocent, 166, 272,
770
intelligence, 693
knowing right and
wrong, 95
maiming, 166
marriage, in, 134
mother and, 690
murder of parents by,
13
negligence towards,
324
only/just a child,
343–344, 742
punishment and, 172,
348
respecting only family,
36
responsible being, as a
, 348
starving, 72, 191, 193,
195, 703
teaching, 676, 787
torturing, 54, 73, 166,
226
unborn, 378, 536,
541–542

Chisholm, Roderick:
attitudinal hedonism
and, 272–273
Brentano and Intrinsic
Value, contribution
in, 276
enjoyment of
non-occurring
events, 267
evaluation of
Chisholm's life, 268
Problem of the
Criterion, 245, 251
Chodorow, Nancy,
722, 727
choice:
between evils (cf
pecca fortiter), 697
consequences of, 697
maximizing, 575
moral, 63, 66, 189,
326, 651, 746,
771, 774
political, 325
power of, 320
problem of, 582
rational, 120, 126,
292, 571, 583–584,
603, 605–606
uncertainty, under,
590
choice situation, 584,
606
Chomsky, Noam, 477
Christian fathers, 635
cigarettes, 194, 280,
365
**circle, looping back in
a (full),** 114, 691,
748
**circles/chains, being
defined,** 707
circumstance:
antecedent, 324, 327

civil society, 441, 564,
569, 723
civilized people, 107
claims, 546
general (moral) claim,
82–83, 347
Clarke, Samuel, 24, 28,
528
class:
cases, of, 376
class of
people/persons,
41, 402, 792
comparison, 35
desires, of, 66
epistemically privileged
, 112
events, of, 327, 405
goods, 702
harmed individuals, of,
408
individuals, of, 408
privileged, 112
progressive, 222
clean slate, 677
clone(-like), 154, 681
close attachments, 691
closeness, 537, 642
Clough, Arthur Hugh,
474
club rule, 139–140, 143
codelike theory,
738–739
coercion:
absense of, 327
agreements and, 514,
579, 597
moral equilibrium, 744
noncoercion, 513
offers they can't refuse
, 513
supererogatory actions
, 533
violence and, 512,

514, 517, 519
coextensiveness, 163,
251, 387, 760
coffee, 121, 139, 543
cognition/ cognitive:
arbitrary, 108
categorical imperative,
492
conviction, 102
economy, 121
epistemology, 740, 745
functioning, 282–284,
643
human reason, of, 489
intrinsic good, 302
intuition, 103–104, 108
non-perceptual, 791
overload, 281
perspective, 281–284
psychotherapy, 277
spontaneity, 121
will, to, 491
cognitivism, 65. *See
also non-
cognitivism;
objectivism/
objectivist*
coherent/ism, 73, 101,
112–115, 121–124
maximally coherent,
119, 595
minimally coherent,
118–119, 125
coin-tossing, 651–652
Coke, Edward, 565
Cold War, 519
Coleman, Jules, 580
Coleman, Linda, 790
collective posterity,
379
color/ colour:
black, 175, 393
blindness, 80–81, 84,

227
blue, 573, 772
green (colour), 227
orange, 52, 99
red, 51, 98, 115, 133,
227, 266, 276,
772, 778, 781
terms, 790
white (colour), 44,
175, 725
yellow, 48–50, 52, 779
command (praecepta),
492
comme il faut, 140, 142
**Commentaries on
Littleton (Coke,
Edward),** 565
commercial pillage,
375
common decency, 477
common humanity,
347, 641–642,
714–715
**common sense (cf
Urteilskraft):**
account, 179
belief, 29
duty, 193
explanations, 182
moral saint, 206
morality, 193–196,
203–205, 764
others, good/ interests
of, 183, 194
values, 203
view, 183, 196
common view, 178,
363, 542, 664, 680
communication:
animal, 367, 370
cross-cultural, 640
instant, 467
moral deliberation, 741
personal, 216

power, 503
process, 694
real opinions, 765
relationship, 694
**compassion and
autonomy,** 695
compatibilism,
306–307, 327, 655
compensating victims,
789
competent user,
221–222
competition:
art, 134
logical, 240
complaisance, 567
**complex action
environment,** 789
complex, the, 52, 302,
445, 529, 631
**compliance (and non-
compliance),** 5,
146–147, 431–432,
434, 438–439, 454,
456, 470, 576–579,
594, 670
comprehensiveness,
118, 125
**compromise
(beeinträchtigen),**
90, 92, 205, 329,
438, 655, 696–697,
747
**compromise
(компромисс):**
children, treatment of,
348
determinism, 346
feminism, 690
generic interpretation,
527
moral bargaining,
39–40
social contract, 555

utilitarianism, 593
compulsion, 141,
320–321, 629
compunction, 347, 758
conation (conative):
ability, 356
commitments, 56
concern, 530
feelings and, 302
interests and, 357, 374
life, 356, 374, 386
limitations, 383
non-conative
conceptions, 152
pursuit, 532
urges, 374
concentration camp,
45, 323
**concepts and
categories,** 790
conceptual absurdity,
374
conceptual equipment,
378
**conclusion of
reflection,** 104
**conclusion/s of
inference,** 55,
103–104
concrete:
particulars, 83
situations, 702, 704,
708, 779
condemnation:
corrupted, 564
determinism, 341
exploitation and hurt,
of, 696
expressing moral, 340
moral, 22, 340–342,
349, 469
positive moral, 22
qualities,
uncontrollable, 326

13

revolutionaries, 306
utility of practices, 350
conditions:
control, of, 323
idealised, 66–67
necessary, 110, 122,
200, 231, 302,
309, 311, 319,
391, 394, 405,
407, 507, 530–532,
583, 599, 620, 741
sufficient, 20, 107,
118, 309–311,
333, 394, 525,
529, 779
conduct requirements,
531
confabulation, 793–794
confederacy, 558, 565
conflict:
duties, 110, 540, 756,
763
interest/s, 107, 541
moral, 649, 692, 695,
768, 770
norms, conflict
between, 692
self and other, 695
conflict resolution,
676, 698
conforming to reason,
138
conformity:
care, with, 696
duty, with, 487–489
Formula of Universal
Law, 509
imperatives, with,
492–493, 500
Kohlberg model, 708
laws, representation of
, 495
noninterfering, 514
past, with the, 634

rational beings, of, 232
reason, to/with,
10–11, 491, 566
reasons for, 163
rule of charity, to, 142
rule-consequentialism,
451
social contract, 723
social rules, 533
superior principle, with
, 7
teaching, 46
universal ends, with,
485
universal law, 488
Confucius, 295
congeries, 310
connectedness,
118–119, 125, 631
connotation, 583, 665,
781. *See also*
denotation
conscience:
borrowing and
repaying, 493
duties, 374, 756
general rules vs, 785
God and, 226
helping beggars, 175
higher faculties, 259
liberty of, 586
moral saints, 201
promptings of, 477
reason, 11
rights, 372
rule- consequentialism,
434
self-deception, 168
softest pillow is a clean
conscience, the,
129
teaching morality, 787
tricking the, 489
utilitarianism, 421

consciousness:
actions, 263
agent's state of,
184–185
animals, 366
attitudinal pleasure,
267
center of, 599
divine, 152
duty, 232
false, 579
FLO, 405
focus of, 186–187
goods of, 403
infants, 378
internal, 260
language, 367
modern moral, 659
moral, 761, 787
necessity, 319
one-caring, 703
pain, 365
reflective, 701
reflective, 701
rights, 390–391
self-, 87, 262, 351,
357, 390, 392,
398, 417, 571
state/s of, 391
streams of, 152
transgression, 232
tried character, 231
virtue, 262
well-being and, 189
what we really think,
761
consensus:
community, 743
free will, on, 56
good, the, 290
intuitionism, 73,
106–107
justifiability of
principles, and, 107

measuring worth, and, 286
metaethical
   commitments, 56
moral values, 693
objective truth, 55
scientific claims, 72
consent:
   achieving ends, 522
   contractualism, 435
   covenant, 566
   equality, 585
   feminist exercise, 748
   higher faculties, to
      resign, 259
   informed, 721
   interference without,
      778, 780
   laws, to, 563
   lying and, 782
   men, of, 568
   mere means, 512
   rules, to, 435
   slavery, to, 587
   spurious, 514
   unforced, 532
consequence/s:
   absurd, 323, 468
   best possible, 760
   choice and, 697
   expected, 414
   ideal calculator of, 683
   language of, 676
consequentialism:
   act- consequentialism,
      413, 416, 431–439,
      450–452, 482,
      484, 753
   attacks on, 184
   collective, 185–187
   conundrum for, 184
   decision procedure,
      677
   definition, 413

demanding nature of,
   415
egoism and, 185
explanatory power,
   189
good, and the, 447
impartiality, 154
impersonal
   benevolence, 690
individual, 185–187
motives and, 660
narrowness, 673
objective, 449–450,
   452–453
pluralism, 661
problem- solving, 676
rule- consequentialism,
   413, 415, 428–439,
   450–451, 457, 767
sophisticated, 184,
   449–450, 456, 763
subjective, 449–450
total causal outcome,
   185
utilitarianism and,
   660–662
varieties of, 185–187
conservation, 242, 372,
   378, 559, 565, 567,
   569–570, 587, 746
conservativism, 121,
   453
consilia, 492
**consistency (and
   inconsistency):**
   appeals to, 787
   evidential, 118, 125
   inconsistency, 26, 96,
      99, 140, 145, 203,
      502, 529, 788
   mutual, 99, 517, 595
   prima facie
      inconsistency, 96

Principle of Generic
   Consistency (PGC),
   529–533
Constant, Benjamin,
   508
**constrained
   maximizers,** 576
constraint:
   agreed, 576, 579
   justified, 572
   overrideable, 522
   side, 482, 521–523
constraints of reality,
   696
construal, 336
consumer society, 472
containment, 505, 519
contentment, 21, 429,
   565–566
contest, 134, 243–244,
   740, 749
context:
   action, of, 510, 516
   comparative, 382
   concrete, 638–639
   context of utterance,
      38
   context- sensitive, 639
   conversational, 57
   cultural, 638
   decision, of, 614
   dependency, 282,
      284, 776, 778
   determinate, 516
   human conduct, 308
   imperatives and, 139
   interpersonal, 86, 343
   moral, 25, 30, 95–96,
      139, 448
   moral concepts and, 32
   moral consideration, of
      , 387
   moral discussion, of,
      200

non-moral, 95. *See also context*
philosophical, 382
political, 86, 163
practical, 87
presocial, 578
public, 455
social, 534
standard, 331
contingency and controversy, 85, 92. *See also outlook*
contingent predilections, 527
contra- suggestibility, 312
contraception, 408–409
contractarianism:
Kant, Immanuel, 556
Rousseau, Jean-Jacques, 556
Why Contractarianism? (chapter 63, Gauthier, David), 571–580
contracts, 43, 134, 376, 524, 526, 560, 562, 628, 720, 723
contractualism:
Contractualism and Utilitarianism (chapter 65, Scanlon, T. M.), 593–608
definition, 435, 598
rejecting, grounds for, 604
contradiction:
Logical, 174, 198, 499, 501–502, 506, 508–509
Practical, 500, 504–509
self-, 98, 180, 198, 292, 489, 530, 534

Teleological, 500, 503–504, 506, 508–509
control:
absence of, 322–323, 336
Control Thesis, 242–245, 251
controversy and contingency, 85, 92
conventions/ conventional, 35, 44, 56, 598, 677, 735, 738–739
actions, 502, 504, 506–507, 683
agreements, 164
beliefs, 415
bravery, account of, 682
conventionalism, 594
cultural relativity and, 598
doctors and, 475
etiquette, of, 35
expression of attitudes, 25
femininity, and, 695
forms, 598
graphic, 280
justice and, 157
Kohlberg's scale, 693
language and, 17–18
moral beliefs and, 682
moral judgments and, 22, 26–27
moral requirements, 164
moral sainthood and, 208
moral standard, 5, 54
moral upbringing and, 682
moral views, 23

morality, 54, 130, 146, 164, 597
murders, on, 407
optimist, 341
political science and, 616
road, of the, 35
rule/s (and), 3, 163–164, 426
social, 6, 44
societal agreement, of, 693
sociocultural context and, 677
truth and, 56
virtue and, 682, 685
converse (logic/ relation):
causality, 319
deficiency, 25
desire to desire, 52
entailment, 23
pleasure and pain, 172
prima facie inconsistency, 96
conversion, 10, 331, 450, 654, 779–780, 783
conviction, 102
contingent factors, shaped by, 85–86
cool, calm and collected, 65–66
corrigibility, 309
corruption/ corrupt, 23, 372, 514, 538, 749
policeman, 524, 527, 533
cosmologist, 96
counsel/s (consilia):
caring, 690, 704
despair, 651
dissenting, 86

empirical, 492
giving, 491–492
perfection, of, 223
Principle of Humanity, 482
prudence, 491
theory, against, 784
wise, 134, 612
counterexample, 74, 88, 287, 521, 738, 744
counterfactual:
assumption, 598
condition, 446, 448, 456
moral predicates, 60
other-regarding, 147, 150
statements, 279, 281
strategic egoism, 157
courage:
acting justly, 514
Aristotle on, 634
communism and, 643
cowardice vs, 25
death, fear of, 636
facing facts, 657, 659
fear vs, 613, 636, 669
force, 134
gallantness, 566
Glaucon, 132
Greeks and, 634
handling situations, 669
Sullivan, 181
target of, 613, 669
temperament, quality of, 485
virtue, 112, 611, 632, 665, 668, 673
covenant, 133, 247, 249, 561–568
cowardly or heroic, 326

craft:
craftsmen, 134, 618
good, the, 615, 617
learning to produce, 622
moral rules, to craft (verb), 753
particular cases, 623
virtues vs, 623
Craig, William Lane, 216, 251–252
God and Objective Morality: A Debate (chapter 25), 225–229
craniotomy, 537
credulity, 91, 678
crime:
attempted murder, 324
bribery, 524, 527, 569
burglary, 546
Dudley and Stephens (necessity no defence to murder), 541
embezzlement, 374, 482
kidnap, 274, 368
Ms. Poore and, 236
murder, 13–14, 36–38, 89, 121, 226, 235, 323–324, 327, 357, 359, 404, 407, 414–415, 420, 437, 470, 475–476, 481, 507–508, 537, 539–540, 548, 625, 630, 648
physical assault, 532
rape, 215, 226–229, 315, 400–401, 414, 434, 717, 720, 733

sexual assault, 731
stealing, 18, 47, 95, 97, 186–187, 235, 239, 320, 356, 432, 436–437, 469, 507, 532, 555, 657, 693–694, 706, 787–789
theft, 236, 239, 420, 482, 625, 694
critical stimuli, 793
cruelty:
animals in sports, 360
animals, to, 359–360, 365–366, 373, 406, 464
attitude towards, 300
caring and, 711
common sense, 95
deliberate/ wilful, 29, 121
God commanding, 220, 223
growth/ development of, 359
hurt without reason, 567
kindness and, 778
mastery of a concept, 779
mixed evil, 272
moral abomination, 226
moral affections, 572
moral vocabulary, 745
pleasures of, 272
right action, theory of, 678
schadenfreude, 271–272
slavery, 464
switching valence, 778
wrongfulness, 224
Cudworth, Ralph, 30,

244, 251
cuisine, 202
**cultural relativism
(CR),** 44–46
curb, 572
curiosity:
anthropological, 572
children and, 289
intellectual, 171, 344
intuitions, 743
knowledge, 301
manipulation and, 429
cutoff point, 393–395,
399
Cyme, 630, 638, 640

D

Daedalus, Stephen,
696
Dancy, Jonathan:
case by case, 435
duties, 754–755
particularism, 435, 672
right-making, 672
thus and so, 672
Unprincipled Morality,
An (chapter 80),
772–775
**Dave (fictitious
character),** 249
**David Copperfield
(Dickens):**
Agnes Copperfield, 202
Betsy Trotwood, 202
de Beauvoir, Simone,
689
dead, the:
ancestors, 372
cremation (vs burial),
97
defamation of, 376
keeping faith with, 376
rights of, 376

death:
abortion, 39, 91, 96,
357–358, 361–362,
369, 390–395,
397–403, 405–409,
536–539, 541–543,
551, 664, 675,
695, 697–698,
703–704, 727. *See
also baby/babies;
infanticide*
accustomed to, 359
attitude toward,
633–634
blame, 323–324
capital punishment
(death penalty),
96, 404, 675,
710–711
child, of a, 467, 537,
541–542, 727
civilian, 483
concentration camps,
457
coneptualizing, 640
covenant, 563
deathbed promise, 648
deserving/
undeserving, 474
desire fulfilment, 295
desire to kill, 396
double effect, 537, 539
duty, 487, 540
dying, classification of,
477
East Bengal, 466
eternal felicity, 566
euthanasia, 369–370,
405, 409, 517,
543, 551
fat man, 537
fear of, 559–560, 636
fear of important
damages, 632

FLO (future like ours),
404
God, of, 225
hysterectomy, 537,
541
infanticide, 44,
390–399, 402,
502, 551, 704. *See
also abortion;
baby/babies;
child/ren,
childhood*
ingratitude, 13
injury amounting to,
541
innocent man, 538–539
intention (direct or
oblique), 538–539,
541
interests after,
376–377
judges and, 538, 540
killing, 403–404
killing vs letting die,
543, 550
knowledge of, 641
lack of necessities,
from, 466–467
Lazarus (Luke
16:24-26), 709
life after death,
234–238, 240
life and death, 186,
409, 438, 477,
510, 674
malnutrition, 193
misfortune, 403–405
mother, 542
natural, 475
negligence, 324
organ donation and,
475
parent, of, 725
patient, 474–475

INDEX TO ETHICAL THEORY: AN ANTHOLOGY

premature, 403–404,
408, 415
promisee, 376
quality of life, 268
remaining time, 357
reputation after, 376
resisting, 563
samsara, 241
side effect, 541
Success Theorists, 295
survival lottery,
474–478
terrorism, 272
violence, 561
whim, 334
wicked merchants, 537
work to death, 243
decalogue. *See ten
commandments
(decalogue)*
decapitation, 309
deceased promisee,
376
deceit, 136, 505
Decembrists, 324
deception:
agreements, 514
compliance, 147
corruption, 514
detecting, 147
false promises, 512
friends and family, of,
414
intentional, 481
justified beliefs, 116
maxims, 512
moral justification, 749
mutual consistency,
517
not knowing about,
271
official line of morality,
143
others as means, 518

self-, 168, 170, 180,
351, 601, 695
test (Kant,
contradiction,
conception), 505
vulnerability to, 513,
519
deciding what to do,
396, 425, 435, 536,
602, 770, 788
decision:
decision making,
formal procedures
of, 697
decision procedure.
See procedure
importing a, 681
life and death, 674
rational, 361
theory, 125
uncertainty, under,
324
Decretum Gratiani, 470
deduction/ deductive:
analogy, narration,
and, 745
argument, 99, 739,
789
computational
(deductive) model,
791
conclusion and
premises, 619
conclusions, 786,
789–790
deductivism, 745–746,
789, 791
explanation, and, 781
inferential relation, 113
kantian, 107
laws of nature and,
569
logic, 529–531, 693
logic canon, 529–531

model, 789–790, 793
moral formulas, 737
optimific acts and, 760
reasoning, 10,
785–786, 790, 793
relations and, 14
right, optimific, and,
761
rules, from, 790,
792–794
support for judgment/s
, 786
use of general
principles, 788, 790
use of moral principles
, 791
validity, 746
vs induction, 112,
529–531, 591–592
deep-self view, 332–338
definable, 17, 49
definition:
agreement, 598
bird, 790
capability of, 50
care, 696
classical, 790–791
contractualism and,
598
contradiction/s and,
501
convention and, 598
CR, 44–45
definitional naturalism,
596
development, 695
dissuasive, 35
ethical concepts, 21
ethical terms, 16
ethics, 707
exceptionless, 779
freedom, 319
good and, 45, 48–49,
280, 285

19

grounding
experience/s, 633
holy, 218–219
horse, 48–49, 52
important duties, 598
intuition/s and, 779
justice, 564–565
lie, 790–791
life, 387
logical constant/s, 174
mathematics, 594
moral relativism, 35
morality, 384, 696, 778
nature of, 52
necessary and
sufficient
conditions, 779
new, 176
ought, 472
particularist/s and, 778
redefinition, 175–176,
332
reducible, 49
reductive, 17
responsibility, 309, 742
rightness, 665
sacrifice, 189
sanity, 335
sexist, 729
soul, body and, 621
stipulative, 176
swan, 175
thick/full definition/s,
632–635
thin/nominal
definition/s,
633–635
true by definition,
174–175
verbal, 49
virtue, 632, 667, 681
deflecting a threat, 548
deity/god, 10, 13, 30,
215–252, 419, 659

authority of, 227, 247,
249
kingdom of god,
232–233, 565
Delian inscription, 620
deliberation:
agent, 151, 309
consequentialist, 449,
451
future, 579
kantian, 516
moral, 144, 387, 612,
689, 742
practical, 86, 154,
207, 209–210
rational, 588
deliberator, 55, 187,
579
delusion, 347, 488
democracy, 227, 461,
736
demogogy, 458
Dennett, Daniel C.,
789, 794
denotation, 48, 50–52,
695. *See also*
connotation
deontology/ ical:
act-, 708
classic, 481
Kantian, 191
language, 442
paradox of, 483
principles, 789
requirements, 482–483
rules, 648–649
theories, 450
utilitarianism and,
645–648
department of enquiry,
99
dependency thesis,
242–245, 251

derivation:
derivatively admirable,
659
relation of, 765
**Descartes, René
(Cartesian),** 365,
367
desert, 162, 216, 240,
273–276, 300–301,
350
desert island, 426, 521
desire/s (Begier):
conflicting, 527, 573,
699
contingent, 148, 529,
532–534
dead, of the, 295
desire to desire, 52
faculty of, 231, 486
rational, 277, 528,
530–531, 533, 602
reciprocity of, 528
theory, 281, 287–290,
292
want and, 491
**determinism/ist
indeterminism/ist:**
actions and, 321
agency and, 310–311
control and, 306
corollary of, 321
Determinism in this
case, 346
falsity of determinism,
305, 341
fear of, 332–333
freedom and, 341
freedom/ free will, and
, 56, 59
indeterminism, 306,
308, 310, 334
indeterminist, 309
knowing what it is, 340

optimism, pessimism,
and, 340–341
outcomes of, 328
problem of
determinism, 305
rationality and, 346
responsibility and,
305–308, 319
soft, 308–309
truth of, 305, 307,
309, 312, 314,
333, 346–347
truth/ falsity of, 338,
340–349
vicarious analogues,
347
we are led back to,
318–319
word, the, 321
development:
arrested, 679
definition of, 695
human, 226
moral, 684, 690,
692–693, 695–696,
722, 728
theories of, 698
virtue/s and, 681
devoted to:
behaving comme il
faut, 142
citizen character, 620
commonplaces, 342
family, 139
hedonism, 255, 272
internalization, 432
Linda, 452
nonmoral interests/
talents, 205
omnipotent, the, 243
other's wellbeing, 658
pursuits, 293
reasoning, 292
dialectic, 102, 373, 490,

698, 764
dictionary, 176, 239,
472
Didion, Joan, 695, 698
die of neglect, 701
diet, 186, 236–237, 368,
523, 636, 663
Dietrichson, Paul, 502,
509
**different voice
(Gilligan, Carol),**
690, 692, 720–723,
727
dignity, 139, 194, 206,
259, 296, 310, 342,
346, 482, 495, 519,
745
dilemma/s:
choice, of, 695
hypothetical, 697
moral, 650–651, 674,
693–694, 697, 723
violence and, 697
diophantine equations,
699
direct applications, 532
disability/ handicap,
147, 166, 227–228,
327, 370, 377, 383,
459, 657–658, 768
**disadvantage (i.e. to
be disadvantaged),**
24, 41, 234, 238,
402, 489, 584–585,
589, 731, 747, 759
disanalogies, 72, 75,
82, 84, 163–164, 635
discourse:
everyday ethical, 677,
684
moral, 455, 695, 742,
747
**discovered rather than
invented,** 227

discrimination:
against gays and
lesbians, 227
brain-damaged
humans over
animals, 356
ethical egoism and,
131
ethnic, 283
grounds for opposing,
362
judgments and, 787
not all bad, 162
racial, 369
racial, 369, 585
racism and sexism,
362
rationality, 278
sex, 729
disparate views, 697
disposition:
coarse-grained, 147
compliant, 147
dispositional
justification, 105
dispositional
understanding, 105
intention, 39
noncompliant, 147
other-regarding, 150
present, 9
rightful, 232
settled, 221
society, of, 587
standing, 451
to act, 299, 326, 449,
597
understanding, 105
vicious, 301
virtue/ virtuous, 261,
299, 668, 684
dissentient moralists,
18
dissentient world, 85

distinguish or disgrace, 326

distribution:
income, of, 586
just, 567, 640, 759
wealth, of, 586

distrust, 51, 115, 143, 196, 455, 568, 701

divergent tastes, 528

divine command, 30, 216–217, 220–224, 229, 232, 248–252, 482

divine designer, 227

divorce, 424

do their part, 40, 42

doctor, 31, 33, 39, 134, 359, 369, 474–477, 540, 621, 623, 710, 726

dogmatism, 46, 107–108, 287, 787

domain:
color terms and natural kinds, of, 790
human, 702
intellectual, 699
metaphysics, of, 495
moral, 62–63, 78–79, 695, 698, 708, 714, 728, 737
moral responsibility, of , 325
public, 702
speculative reason, of, 232
strictures of relevant domains, 163

doom, 239, 648, 696

Dostoyevsky, Fyodor, 251

double effect, 399, 483–484, 536–539, 541–542, 551

doubt:
problem of, 789

drawing straws, 547

Driver, Julia, 670, 675

drivers (motorists):
reckless, 306, 323
steering, 538–540
truck, 324

drug/s:
analgesic/ pain- killing, 294, 297
color perception altering, 772
contentment- inducing (soma), 429
depressive, 392
drink, cigarettes and, 194
hallucinogenic, 781
induced hallucination, 116
mind-impairing, 330
psychoactive, 265
scarce, 539–541
sex, drugs and rock 'n' roll, 270
stealing medicine for family, 692–694

drunken beggar, 527

drunkenness, 46, 135, 306, 324, 527, 569

Dudley and Stephens (necessity no defence to murder), 541

Duncan-Jones, Austin, 177

duty/duties (Pflicht):
absolute, 758, 760, 768
actual, 383, 494, 500, 755, 757–759, 761
apathy and self-mastery, of, 207
basic, 764–768, 770
basic rights and, 581
beneficence, 102, 515, 757, 763–764, 766–769
beyond the call of, 415, 785
conditional, 376, 757–758
conflict of, 110, 540, 756, 763
conflicting, 107, 110, 540, 763
consequential, 757
contractual, 767
custodial, 374
derivative, 766
fidelity, 102, 111, 598, 764–766, 768
final, 107, 109
gratitude, 102, 757, 764–767
imperfect, 206, 493, 513
instrumental, 60
justice, 301, 515, 757, 764, 766, 768
legal, 373
motive of, 159, 326, 418
negative, 146, 396–397, 540, 544–545, 551
positional, 767
positive, 146, 151, 206, 396, 540–541, 544–545, 551
prima facie, 38, 102–103, 106–109, 546, 702, 754, 757–766

prima facie duties
(Ross), 102,
108–109, 546,
702, 751, 754,
757–758, 760–761,
764–766, 768, 770
primary, 757
principles of, 103,
106, 108, 489,
759–760, 771
proper, 757, 764, 769
putative basic, 766–767
ranking of, 768
reparation, 757
rule of, 139, 418
self- improvement,
757, 764, 768
stringent, 768
unconnected heap of,
754, 763
underivative, 764, 766
universal imperative of
, 493
veracity, 765
Dworkin, Gerald, 755
Unprincipled Ethics
(chapter 82),
785–794
dying before birth, 378

E

economic systems, 730
education:
level of, 536
well-educated, 102,
761
Edwards, Paul, 308,
311
effect/ effects:
double, 399, 483–484,
536–539, 541–542,
551
ntypicality, 790

side, 541
egalitarian, 162, 526,
528, 530, 535, 606,
669, 674, 680
egoism:
consequentialist,
183–187
ethical, 130–131,
145–149, 157,
161–163, 189,
192, 690, 755
Ethical Egoism
(chapter 21,
Rachels, James),
193–199
Flourishing Egoism
(chapter 20, Hunt,
Lester), 178–192
Psychological Egoism
(chapter 19,
Feinberg, Joel),
167–177
rational, 149–153,
161–163, 166, 556
egoist:
anti-, 162
disagreeing with, 91
discriminatory
treatment, 162
ethical, 146–150, 156,
195, 198
fairness, 582
Kantianism vs, 483
metaphysical, 145,
152–157
moral saint, 203
Nietzsche, 658
psychological, 177
Rand, Ayn, 183
rational, 149–152,
157, 161–163, 166
strategic, 147, 154
theories, 179

egoistic:
bias, 715
ethics, 195
generosity, 658
generosity, 658
hedonism, 171,
184–185, 204, 444
policies, 195
psychological egoistic
hedonism, 167, 170
self-interest, 658
self-interest, 717
egotism, 21
Einstein, Albert, 708
Ellington, James, 158,
509
emotion:
abortion, 704
altruistic, 717
animal, 366–367
appeal, 395
Aristotle on, 670–671
attachment, 289
aversion, 7–8
balance, 392
birth and upbringing,
58
brain and, 366
care-givers, 737
cognition, 284
contrarianism, 727
De Sousa on, 794
distress, 279
disturbance, 391
duty, 717
experience, 737
expression, 4, 16
future, 704
heat of, 710
incorrect, 272
intellect over, 726
interactions, history of,
742
Klein on, 642

mind, 9
moral, 313
moral importance of, 777
moral standing, 356
needs, 723
Noddings on, 690
objective attitude, 344
objective values, 26
objects and, 8
outbursts, 65
paradigm cases, 792
power, 186
propensity, 7–8
rational control of, 727
reason, 9
responses, 4
sensible, 9
social construction, 636
stability, 164
tightrope walker, 187
training, 292, 651
violent, 9
virtue, 671
women and, 689–690
emotivism, 19, 84, 98, 221, 594, 705–707
emphasis, 95
patterns of, 738
substance and, 721
empiricism/ empirical, 18, 28, 107–108, 350, 441
belief, 58, 72, 86–87
hypotheses, 16–17, 173–176. *See also hypotheses based on*
propositions, 17–18
theory, 75–76, 79
enabling, 539
sentiment, 699
stories, 746

enchantments, 135
end game, 373
end of our species, 379
endowment, 14, 206, 259, 265, 306, 362, 419, 583, 642, 704
ends and means, 521–522, 536
enemy, 12, 36–37, 42, 134–135, 237, 420, 422, 483, 488, 558–560, 563, 565, 590, 605–606, 624, 780
enlightened conscience, 372
Enlightenment, 778, 780
entailment, 23, 29
entitlements, 510, 735
envy. *See jealousy/envy*
eo instante, 565
Epictetus, 191
epicureanism, 192, 258
epistemic:
defeater, 57, 62
dependence, 105
duty, 60
fact, 60
justification, 112
principle, 60–61, 108–109
privilege, 112–116, 123–124
epistemology:
approach to, 455
compatible, 594
critical, 740, 747
enjoyment, of, 267
feminist, 735–736, 740, 750
intuitionistic, 674
moral, 6, 71, 73, 106, 24

595, 691, 716, 735–736, 741, 744
naturalized, 740, 750
normative
epistemology, 741
equal share, 696
equality:. *See also inequality*
animals, 361–371
argument for, 361
blacks, 362
egoism, 163
factual, 362
God, existence of, 226
inequality, 162, 299, 564, 568, 583, 586–587, 606, 631, 633, 696–698, 726–727, 736
legal, 407
liberty and, 519
logic of equality and reciprocity, 697
material, 519
moral, 363, 689
natural, 568
opportunity, of, 587
original position of, 581
other-regarding, 149
pretense of, 726
principle of, 362–363, 365, 368
rationally grounded, 532
virtual, 726
women, 361, 689
equation, 693, 695–696, 699
equilibrium:
reflective, 150, 273, 436, 573, 579, 585, 743, 745, 750
equity, 528, 567–569

equivocation, 41–42,
148, 175
Erikson, Erik, 693, 696,
698
Eros (Ερως), 699
Eskimos, 97
eternity, 7, 231–232
ethics/ethical (Ethik):
adult, 696
aspirations, 683
care, of, 690,
695–696, 698,
723–724, 749
environmental, 387
feminist, 687–750
ideal, 167, 700–702,
704, 707, 710–711
mathematics and, 34
medical, 721
methods of, 27, 298,
457, 473, 534,
785, 794
naturalism, 6, 50–51
nonnaturalism, 6,
54–55, 57, 59, 61
normative, 18, 166,
276, 551, 611,
649–652
observation and, 31,
33
philosophy and, 60, 62
relativism, 5, 612
sentiment, 699, 709
statements, 16–19, 28
theological, 30. See
also
virtue, 435, 611–613,
631, 638, 643,
645–657, 659,
661, 663–664,
667, 673–676,
680–685, 719
recent revival of,
15

ethnocentric, 676
etiology, 116
etiquette, 35, 47, 60,
130, 139–143,
148–150, 156,
163–164, 705

Europeans, 313, 641
euthanasia:
active, 405
greater happiness, 517
killing and letting die,
543, 551
legitimacy, 369
evaluation:
action or, 165
acts, of, 664
agents, of, 653, 664
basis for, 159
desires, 287, 292
judgment and, 322
lives, of, 268, 272, 274
moral, 120, 160, 164,
166, 208, 384,
654–655, 660
motivations, of, 207
reevaluations, 454
reflection and, 292
self-, 337
state of the world, of a
, 327
thoughts and, 185
worlds, of, 274
Evans, Jonathan St. B.
T., 794
everyday (ethical)
rules, 677
evidence:
assessment of, 85, 88,
90
behavioural, 366
beliefs and, 123, 125
connections, 112
relations, vs, 123

consistency, 118, 125
counter-, 175
degree of, 12
divided, 107
empirical, 56, 168,
171, 174, 786
errors and, 124
evidential/ inferential
relations, 112–113,
115, 118, 122
experience and,
122–123
experimental, 794
hypotheses based on,
27, 175. See also
hypotheses
independent, 88
intuitions as, 74–76,
79. See also
intuition/s (cf
Anschauung,
intuitus)
observational, 32–34,
75, 103, 786
positive, 116
probative, 166, 309
question- begging and,
58
relations and, 125
self-, 73, 102–106,
109, 585, 754, 759
sensory/ perceptual,
4, 28, 55, 58,
76–78, 122, 173,
778, 790, 794. See
also senses
tautologies and, 175
textual, 501, 770
evidential consistency
requirement, 125
evil (mala, böse):. See
also wicked/ ness
aversion to, 9

avoiding, 652
bad will, 322
balancing, 287, 541
Beyond Good and Evil
    (Nietzsche), 315,
    658
choice between, 697
competitor, 244
consequence, 561
deep self, 336
demon, 86–87, 116,
    778
dictator, 334
distinguishing, 10–13,
    489, 528
duty, 489
established morality
    and, 23
existing morality, 749
explanations and, 123
genocide, 165
God and, 243–244
good and/or evil,
    10–13, 94,
    242–244, 300,
    315, 336, 538,
    541, 569, 658,
    759, 762, 794
good will, 485
Hitler and, 37
immunity from, 507
inactivity, 468
infant awareness of,
    722
inflicting, 647–648
injustice, 721
inner judgments and,
    36–37
instrumental, 191
intention, 537–538
internalism, 160
intrinsic, 245
killing and saving, 769
Lazarus and, 709

lesser, 226, 563
lying promise, 492
mixed, 272
Nazi, 782
objective truth, 23
one-caring, 710
ought vs, 37
pain, 370
power, 244
preventable, 468
punishment, 161
relativism and, 36
responsibility, 333
restraint, 786
revenge and, 9, 567
scarcity and, 674
size of, 541
slavery, 461
suffering, 134, 617
torturing animals,
    398, 678
transcendant
    expediency, 420
trolley, 547
turning from, 546
unworthy object,
    272–274
vice, 569
violence, 311
virtue, 667
voluntas vs cupidas,
    528
evolution, 226–227,
    250, 366, 384, 695,
    794
ex ante, 577–578, 787
ex hypothesi, 312, 476,
    651
excellence/s, 202, 204,
    206, 247, 457, 627,
    664, 666–667, 672,
    678
excuses, 209, 322, 421,
    729

exemplar, 55, 611, 742,
    779–780, 791
exemplary moral
    agent, 690
exile, 295, 706
existentialism, 26, 735
expediency, 89, 420,
    424, 583, 623
experience (cf
    Erfahrung):
    cause and effect and,
        13
    common, 10, 642
    conscious, 298
    crucial emphasis for
        change, as, 121
    grounding, 123,
        633–637, 640–641
    impetus for change, as
        , 121
    importance of, 121
    influence of, 90
    justified beliefs and,
        114–115
    moral, 16, 595, 600,
        713, 718–719,
        735, 739, 774
    neuromanipulator and,
        87
    private, 116
    relations of objects
        and, 7–8
    upbringing and, 88–89
    values shaped by, 85
experimental subjects,
    790
expert, 53, 55, 99, 366,
    467, 472, 486, 514,
    624, 680–683, 685,
    780
explaining
    observations, 33,
    571

explanatory:
chain, 34
claim to be, 60
deduction, induction,
abduction and/or,
112
epistemically, 103
hypotheses, 27
notion, 103
obligation, 77
reasons, 150
requirement, 122
role, 34, 574–575
task, 79
theory, 34, 722
exploitation, 102, 696,
724, 726, 736
exposition, 130, 267,
404, 424, 482, 586,
764
**expressive-
collaborative
model,** 741–744,
746
expressivism, 84
external world, 94–99,
675
externalism, 116, 122,
161

F

facelessness, 379
fact/s:
matters of, 4, 14, 96,
174, 260, 301, 363
mistake of, 11, 290
natural, 29, 107
non-evaluative, 235,
296
physical, 33, 60
putative (moral), 5, 61
logical, 97, 235,

total, 300–301
fairness:
alternative
distributions, 429
care and, 698
compliance, 147
devotion to, 207
egocentric
understanding of,
693
equality and
reciprocity, 693
goal fulfillment, 696
intrafamilial justice and
, 672
intrinsic value, 415
intuitive standard of,
577
justice as fairness,
556, 581–584, 591
moral evaluation, 159,
166
moral life, in, 482–483
mutual, 745
obligation, 145
other-regarding, 149
primitive sense of, 792
procedural, 578, 602
reciprocal, 534
respect and, 133
rightness as, 584
rule- consequentialism,
430
societal agreement,
693
students, to, 86
taxation, 519
virtue ethics, 612
weight, 430
well-being and, 430,
435
faith:
bad faith, 93, 449, 775
general, 424, 426

good faith, 142, 546
keep faith, 100, 376
moral order, in, 427
rational, 232
religious, 314
fallacy:
ad hominem, 652, 758
analytic and synthetic
arguments, and,
169
definist, 384
determinism, and, 319
disinterested
benevolence, 169
equivocation, 227
genetic, 227
naturalistic (G. E.
Moore), 50–52, 384
pathetic, 29–30
reason vs passion, 7
suppressed correlative,
176
false contrast, 765
false witness, 757
falsifiability, 175, 506
family:
animals and, 369
bereavement, 403
concern for, 153
contempt, 271
deception, 271, 414
devotion to, 139
divorce, 424
fair shares, 672
fairness, 698
family first, 448
Gauguin, 324
ground projects, 447
Harvey, 427
interdependence, 689
involuntary
membership, 690
leaving home, 687
love, 237, 270

marginal utility, 471
obligation to, 154,
  717–718
overlapping groups,
  46, 641–642
partiality, 438
patriarchal, 732
promises, 718
relationships, 698
respecting, 36
responsibilities, 42,
  689, 715, 743, 745
right and wrong,
  teaching, 705
shame, 313
stealing medicine for,
  692–694
unequal infant, 727
victimless crimes, 482
virtue, 676
fat man:
  heavy, 545, 549–550
  stuck, 537, 541
fate:
  accident of, 86
  contributions of, 325
  cruel, 464
  divine, 620
  formidable, 478
  indignant about, 487
  mercy of, 326
  opportunities
    determined by, 476
  others, of, 487
  prisoner of, 321
  religion's apparent fate
    , 574
  same, the, 364
  terrible, 136
  unfortunate, 322
  world, of the, 450
Father Knows Best,
  201

fathers:
  absent, 708
  accusation of, 564
  action, 206
  care-takers of, 710
  Christian, 635
  dead, 336
  domestic responsibility
    , 725
  Father Brown
    (Chesterton), 202
  Father Knows Best,
    201
  godfather, 255
  grandfather, 549
  harsh, 709
  head, as, 725
  occupation, 693
  reason, 622
  sons, and, 135, 243
  special feelings, 334
  unchosen, 724
  violent, 727
favoritism, 572
feelings:
  appeal to, 573
  approval, of, 17
  attitudes and, 350
  certain feelings under
    certain
    circumstances, 326
  convictions and, 223
  desires and, 29
  estimable, 259
  excitants of, 19
  expressions of, 4, 16,
    19, 21, 65,
    331–332, 642
  following one's, 616
  guilt, 313, 432
  hurting, 47
  inclinations and, 139
  judgment and, 260
  moral, 39, 223, 418

morality, about, 141
nature of, 17
nobler, 260
others, of, 278
our own, 20
ourselves, about, 327
pleasure as, 266–268
propositions about, 19
read our, 29
reports of, 23
retrospective, 328
special, 334
sympathetic, 572
tone and, 18
Feinberg, Joel:
  introduced, 130, 356
  moral considerability,
    on, 385
  moral responsibility,
    on, 325
  Psychological Egoism
    (chapter 19),
    167–177
  Rights of Animals and
    Unborn
    Generations, The
    (chapter 44),
    372–380
Feldman, Fred,
  256–257, 407, 409
  Good Life: A Defense
    of Attitudinal
    Hedonism, The
    (chapter 266),
    266–276
fellow-feeling, 695
fellows, our, 572, 757.
  See also other(s)
feminine goodness,
  696
feminine voice, 695
feminism. *See feminist*
Ferguson, Adam, 727
fertility, 695

fiction, 99, 202, 376, 517, 592, 596, 757

fidelity:

agreements, to, 598, 754

fairness and, 612

promises, to, 301, 761

right, is, 755

Fillmore, Charles, 790

final sentence, 699

First Nations, 676

fitness (fit,fittingness):

arbitrator, 568

attaining proposed ends, 485

eternal/ immutable, 10, 12

intuition of fittingness, 341, 350, 596

moral values/ valuing, 22–23

natural, 13

reasonable, and, 24

relations, 28–29

Five Ws (+ similar terms):

how, the, 105

that, the, 105, 776, 783

what, the, 105

why, the, 776, 783

flourishing (eudaimonia/ eudæmonia/ ευδαιμονία):

Abelard, and, 178

eudaimonia, 611

Flourishing Egoism (chapter 20, Hunt, Lester), 178–192

human, 286, 444, 631, 638, 641

~~131, 612,~~
~~0~~

problems of, 640

search for, 641

state, 670

foetus, 536–537, 542

Fool/ Foole, 97, 191, 243, 259, 556, 565, 576–577

Foot, Philippa:

Analogical Argument, The, and, 163

Are Moral Considerations Overriding?, 241

introduced, 6, 129, 483–484

morality and etiquette, 149

Morality as a System of Hypothetical Imperatives (chapter 16), 138–143

negative vs positive duties, 551

Problem of Abortion and the Doctrine of the Double Effect, The (chapter 60), 399, 536–542

torturing five men vs one, 539, 548

trolley problem, 544–545

villains, 548

virtues, the good life, 631

for its own sake:

acquisition of knowledge, 171

allowing sth to happen, 539

commitment, 444

concern for future self, 155

deserving to be valued, 386

desire, happiness, 261

discovering what is worth desiring, 255

duty, doing one's, 481

God commanding cruelty, 220, 223

good, 132

intrinsic pleasure, 269

pain alleviation, 165

pigs, welfare of, 170

power, 290

rational agency, 151

tennis, 445

virtue (& acts of), 237, 262, 666

wealth/money, 446

for the most part, 755, 780–782

for their own sake, 132, 141, 151, 154–155, 157, 171, 194, 203, 256, 373

force:

claims, of, 150

evidential, 82

habit, of, 263

intuitive, 78

magic, 142

mesmeric, 30

moral, 602

physical, 322, 733

reason-giving, 140, 165–166, 778

regress argument, of the, 114

scope and, 314

forebodings, 115, 117

forgiveness, 136, 307, 342, 344, 563, 742

formalism, 596

fortunate act, 759

INDEX TO ETHICAL THEORY: AN ANTHOLOGY

fortune:
good, 460, 510, 611,
620, 759
ill, 632
misfortune, 135,
403–406, 408,
476, 478, 491,
617, 620, 632, 723
Foucault, Michel,
636–637, 641
foundationalism:
bankrupt project/
discredited,
573–574
coherentism and,
112–117, 122
epistemic privilege,
115
epistemological, 101
externalism, 116
extramoral foundations
, 573–574
intuitionism, 110
justification, 113, 116
normative, 573
promise-keeping, 101
regress, 115, 123
self-evident, 101
**Frankena, William
Klaas,** 384–385,
389, 443, 711
Frankfurt, Harry,
331–334, 337, 339,
580
fraternity, 722
**Fred and Jane
(fictitious
characters),**
680–681
freedom:. See also
liberation;
libertarian/ism;
liberty

action, of, 331, 394,
497, 760
assembly, of, 586
Freedom and
Necessity (chapter
38, Ayer, A. J.),
317–321
Freedom and
Resentment
(chapter 41,
Strawson, Peter),
340–352
interference, from, 690
moral condemnation/
punishment, 341
moral responsibility,
341
speech, of, 85, 586
thought, 641
well-being, 529–532
will, of the, 315, 317,
319, 321, 326,
331, 339
Freud, Sigmund, 294,
642, 692, 695
friend/ship:
abandoning a stranded
, 107
agent-neutrality, 150,
156
agent-relativity, 156
another-self, 157
associations of, 153
betrayal of, 649
character, 191
good of, value in the,
191
happiness, 447
human needs and
desires, 642
intrinsic value, 413
loaning cars, 249
love for, 668

maximizing pleasure,
429
maximizing pleasure,
429
motivation, 717
normative account,
638
objectivism, 429
ought, 446
personal attachments,
186
sophisticated hedonist,
445
tensions, 86
transfers, 561
upbringing, and, 92
virtue, 153, 645, 668
wallet, 186–187
fruit:
apple, 11, 399
banana, 662
bearing fruit through
effort, 519
Homer on, 135
labor, of, 558
lemons, 52, 99
misjudging, 11
oranges, 52, 99
relish, as, 9
uncertain, 559
Frye, Marilyn, 691
Sexism (chapter 76),
729–734
**full-information
theory,** 277–281
future:
deliberation, 579
Future Like Ours (FLO)
, 403–408
generations, 372,
378–380, 726–727
good, 289, 403
interests, 151, 378–379

pleasure and good, 403
fuzzy boundaries, 790

G

Gage, Francis D., 371
gain-and-loss table, 590–591
Galbraith, John Kenneth, 473
Galileo Galilei, 96
Galt, John, 181, 190
game/s:
  board, 163
  card, 381
  Cheat, 765
  chess, 791–792
  competitive, 555
  devotion to the, 445
  Diplomacy, 782
  end game, 373
  game theory, 454
  golf, 203
  habits and, 185
  imperial war, 461
  incurring guilt, and, 249
  morality game, 164
  play the game, 696, 724
  pleasant, 136
  pushpin, 255
  requirements/ rules, 164, 693
  strategy, 590
  structured, 737
  tennis, 184, 445
Gandhi, Mohandas Kamarchand, 210, 680
  ⌐ance, 378

character), 541
Gauguin, Paul, 324, 328
Gauthier, David, 556–557
  Why Contractarianism? (chapter 63), 571–580
Gaylin, Willard, 709
gays and lesbians, 227, 637
gender:
  bias, 690, 713–714, 718–719, 736, 739, 749
  caretaker's gender, 722
  categories, 719
  cultural commonplaces, 740
  differences (moral outlook), 727
  gender feminists, 91
  homosexual experience, 637
  human differences, 715
  inequality, 736
  Justice, Care, and Gender Bias (chapter 74, Calhoun, Cheshire), 713–720
  moral skills lacked, 727
  neutrality, 713, 719, 722
  personality differences, 722
  powers distribution of, 736
  right to life, 401
  rights and responsibilities study, 692
  roles, 719, 743

sensitivity/ insensitivity, 719
sex-marking, 734
sexism, 690
sexual appetite, 636
social divisions, 739
social life, 736
substantial differences/ similarities, 715
general conception, 104, 586–587
generalization:
  codifiable, 783
  criterial, 786
  defeasible, 755, 782–783
  defensible, 783
  explanatory, 778, 780, 784
  quasi-, 786
  theoretical, 778–780, 782–783
  universal, 175
generation/s:
  future, 372, 378–380, 726–727
  next, 372, 726
  previous, 589
  unborn, 372–373, 375, 377, 379, 389
generosity:
  agent needs, 659
  alleviating need, 669
  bourgeois, 638
  breaking one's word, 564
  causal power, 59
  duty vs charity, 469–470
  egoistic, 658
  grounds to deny, 669
  intermediate state, 626
  interpretation, 778

money, 625
motivation, 130
reputation, 660
self-sufficiency,
    658–659
sharing scarce
    resources, 778, 782
transformations, 643
virtue, 622, 632, 637,
    665, 671
genetic:
engineering, 433
genetically modified
    food, 665
policy, 588
genocide, 3, 72, 165,
    406. *See also*
    Holocaust
Gensler, Harry, 5–6
Cultural Relativism
    (chapter 6), 44–47
genus, 49, 54–55, 624,
    777
Gewirth, Alan, 483
Golden Rule
    Rationalized, The
    (chapter 59),
    524–535
Gide, André, 316
Gierke, Otto, 591
Gilligan, Carol, 690,
    708, 712–713, 717,
    719–728, 749
In a Different Voice
    (chapter 72),
    692–698
giving, 356, 437, 453,
    469, 471
giving alms, 757, 769
for the praise of men,
    141
giving permission, 539
**Glaucon (elder
    half-brother of**

Plato), 129, 132,
    134–137, 572. *See
    also Adeimantus
    (elder half-brother
    of Plato)*
global village, 467
goal-directed, 522
god. *See deity/god*
god among humans,
    133
godfather, 255
godless doctrine, 419
gold ring. *See Ring of
    Gyges*
**Golden Rule (Mt 7:12,
    Lk 6:31),** 47, 168,
    197, 417, 465,
    482–483, 524–535,
    569, 601, 689, 787
Rational Golden Rule,
    530–531, 533–534
Golding, Martin, 794
Goldstein, Laurence,
    794
good and/or evil:
balance of, 538, 541
desert or moral, 300
distinguishing, 10–13,
    489
existence of, 242–243
God's creative activity,
    242
intrinsic, 244–245
knowledge of, 94
mind and, 12
moral philosophy, 569
power, 244
private appetite, 569
reason and, 11
universally
    acknowledged, 13
weighing up, 538

will/ pleasure of God,
    244
good excuse, 107
Good Samaritan, 787
good woman, 695
**good/Good, (The)
    (bona),** 30
balance of, 541,
    769–770
bonum consummatum
    (deserved/ realized
    good), 300
conditional, 117
future, 289, 403
general, 417, 761, 765
good, common, 724
good, intrinsic/ally,
    244–245, 255,
    257, 263, 286,
    299, 302, 387
good/s, public, 147
goods, complex, 302
greater, 131, 260,
    437, 453, 583, 598
greatest, 137, 247,
    286, 521, 611
maximize/ maximum,
    415–416, 761
non- subtractive, 532
premoral, 702
primary, 587, 591
summum bonum
    (highest/ supreme
    good), 230–233
surplus of, 769
the good life,
    266–267, 269,
    271, 273, 275,
    277, 631, 719, 786
units of, 436, 760
Goodall, Jane, 367
Goodman, Nelson,
    592, 639, 644
goodness, 702

Goodpaster, Kenneth, 356
On Being Morally Considerable (chapter 45), 381–389
goods:
additive, 532
non- subtractive, 532
goody-goody, 203
Gopalan, Coluthur, 644
Gore, Al, 662
Gough, John Wiedhofft, 591
Grant, James (UNICEF), 193
gratitude (and ingratitude):
antecedent grace, 567
Aristotelian virtue, 642
ass and the bell, the, 360
beneficiary/ benefactor, to, 414, 761
benevolence, 567
duty, 102, 757, 764–767
good, 569
ingratitude, 13, 567, 569
John, Anne, Lisa, Helen (fictitious characters), 442
justification, 60
philanthropy, 170–171
reactive attitude, 752
reasons, 247
resentment and, 342–344
transacting, 342
gravediggers, 537
gravitation, 758

greatest(-) happiness principle, 258, 417, 510
Green, Thomas Hill, 152, 157, 230
Greene, Theodore M., 509
Gregoire, Henry, 371
Gregor, Mary, 210, 485, 728
Grice, Geoffrey Russell, 592
Griffin, James Patrick, 294, 371
Gross National Product (GNP), 472
Grotius, Hugo, 725
ground/s:
act-utilitarian, 415
affectional, 92
against moral objectivism, 164
against self-love, 195
against virtue ethics, 645
agent - person connection, of, 394
ascribing the right to life, for, 397
assumptions of knowledge, for, 338
aversion to pain, for, 291
belief, for, 116, 121
believing one is right, for, 93
causal thinking, for, 191
circumvent survival lottery, to, 476
conceptual, 109
concluding intent for an action, for, 396
contingent, 495

contractualist, 596, 602, 606
defending preferences, for, 282
defensibility of actions, for, 602
denying animals the right to life, for, 395
denying pain felt by animals, for, 367
desires, for, 289
discounting, for, 591
disinterested, 231
disqualification of rights of animals, for, 373
distinctions, for, 116
doubt, for, 87
drawing parallels with scientific method, for, 677
duty, of, 107
empirical, 103
environmental inheritance, of, 372
evolutionary, 75
extreme utilitarian, 424
faulting justice, for, 132
geographical, 467
God's authority, of, 247
greater good, of, 583
hedonic, 107
inductive, 119
inferential, 105–106
inferring lack of other motives, for, 172
interests (interest principle), of, 377
intuitive/ intuitionist, 106, 596

justifying one's
actions, of,
600–601, 607
Kantian, 355
knowing/ knowledge,
of, 103, 107–108
knowledge about, 103
libertarian rights, for,
146
limiting definitions, of,
175
love, of, 157
mathematical
judgment, of, 594
medical, 541
moral, 107, 453
moral judgments, for,
88, 325
moral rationalism,
against, 163
opposing
discrimination, for,
362
projects, 202, 447, 453
prudential, 476
public conception of
justice, for a, 589
punishment, for, 521
question- begging, 58
racism, for, 199
rational, 91, 788
rejecting
contractualism, for,
604
rejecting discussion,
for, 425
rejecting ethical
egoism, for, 189
rejection of
alternatives, for,
121, 597
religious, 651
Ross, DAIAH, and, 274

seeking others'
well-being, for, 183
self-interest, 139
skepticism, for, 79, 94
species- specific
impossibility of care
reciprocity, for, 703
statistical, 91
strong, 703

theoretically simple,
677
to deny generosity,
669
to reject NAFTA, 662
to reject premises, 236
truth, of, 594
utilitarian, 460, 476,
596
utilitarianism, for, 120,
597, 600
virtue, of, 238
what happens, for, 495
grounding:
deficiency, 637
experience, 123,
633–637, 640–641
justification for
substantive truths,
108
justificatory grounding,
767
perspective, 209
premises, 106
rational desires, 528
relations, 110
Gute, das, 300
Gyges of Lydia, 133,
157

H

Haan, Norma, 694
Habermas, Jürgen,

579–580
habitual ascendancy,
320
habituation, 611,
619–620, 622–623
Hackforth, Reginald,
158
Hall of Holograms, 782
Hamilton, Edith, 158
Hampshire, Stuart,
477–478, 777, 784
hands-off policy, 690
happy/ unhappy(ness):
accidents, 203
businessman, 270
children, 171, 274, 294
desiring one's own,
138
producing, 205
Haraway, Donna, 740,
750
**hardness of heart
(σκληροκαρδία),**
284–285, 547
Hare, Richard Mervyn,
27, 40, 43, 239,
415–416
What is Wrong with
Slavery (chapter
52), 458–465
harm:
causing, 668, 765
inclination to, 757
Harman, Gilbert:
causal test of
ontological
credibility, 59
ethical relativism, 5
Ethics and Observation
(chapter 4), 31–34
Hitler, on, 145
Hume, on, 5
introduced, 5

INDEX TO ETHICAL THEORY: AN ANTHOLOGY

Is There a Single True
Morality?, 158
moral facts, 59, 61–62
Moral Philosophy
Meets Social
Psychology, 685
Moral Relativism
Defended (chapter
5), 35–43, 145, 158
Nature of Morality,
The, 126
nihilism, 571, 580
Harris, John, 416
Survival Lottery, The
(chapter 54),
474–478
Harsanyi, John C., 573,
602, 604–605
Hart, H. L. A., 309, 371,
536–537, 542
harvesting, 134, 512,
576
hate, 91, 218, 272, 291,
326, 543, 678, 701,
710
heads may be counted,
96
Health-Pebble, 546–550
healthy soul, 572, 657
**heaven and hell
(hades),** 135–136,
313–314
hedonic, 107, 386, 777
inclinations, 527
hedonism/ist:
Desert- Adjusted
Intrinsic Attitudinal
Hedonism (DAIAH),
273–275
Double Desert-
Adjusted Intrinsic
Attitudinal
Hedonism
(DDAIAH), 275

egoistic, 171, 184–185
Intrinsic Attitudinal
Hedonism (IAH),
269–271
Narrow, 294
paradoxical, 171,
444–446
pleasure and, 173,
266, 268, 294, 387
Preference, 294–297
psychological, 142,
170, 172–173
psychological egoistic,
167, 170
sensory, 268, 270
sophisticated, 445–446
Veridical Intrinsic
Attitudinal
Hedonism (VIAH),
271–272
**Hegel, Georg Wilhelm
Friedrich
(Hegelian),** 152,
157–158, 724–725
**Heinz (fictitious
character),** 692–694
Helen of Troy, 626
hell (hades), 135–136,
313–314
heredity, 312, 332
hermit-monk, 702
Hesiod, 135, 137, 617
Bear acorns at the top
and bees in the
middle, 135
Vice in abundance is
easy to get, 135
heteronomy, 232
heuristic, 589, 780
high fashion, 202
high wall, 136
Himmler, Heinrich, 160

historical:
agent-basing, 654
alienation, reasons for,
441
allegiances, 777
authoritative
representations,
736
awareness, 351
change, 637
conditions
(non-necessary),
637
counter examples, 173
differences, 636

expressive-collaborative
model, 741
Fountainhead, The
(Rand, Ayn), 181
generalization, 178
Gough, J. W. survey,
592
hedonism, importance
of, 255
influences, 81
moral philosopher, 739
moral responsibility,
313
non-arbitrary context,
638
original position, 581
outdated religious
views, 81
outlook origins, 91
practices, 455
product, 454
slavery, books on, 459
social contract theory,
antecedents of, 555
veil of ignorance, 725
virtue and self-interest
, 178

World War II,
accounts of, 281

history:
accident of, 86
agent's, 338
Aristotle in the light of, 635
attention to, 454
beliefs without, 116
causality, 310, 320
civilizing virtues, 168
concrete, 631
contrived, 203
determinism,
controversy, 338
disagreement on, 27
ethics, of, 659
evolutionary, 81, 366
female exclusion, 689
fiction vs, 757
Greek thought, 636
History of Sexuality
(Foucault, Michel), 636, 641
human ignorance
throughout, 76–77
hypothetical dilemmas, 697
influence on beliefs, 86, 89–91
interactions, of, 742
intuitionism, 72
Judaeo- Christian-
Kantian construct, 313
judge, as, 387
knowledge of, 459
language change, 455
mind, the human, 639
moral argument, 67
moral decisions, 746
moral standing, 356
objectivity, 98
paradigmatic, 498

past cases, 780
perspective and
cognitive state, 282
philosophy, 53, 58, 293
postmodernism, 741
recording changes/
events, 456
retroactive justification, 325
rights, conferring, 546
shared in relationships, 444
slavery, 463–464
unreliable theorizing, 741
women's oppression, 725

Hitler, Adolf:
Cultural Relativism, 44
Harman, Gilbert, on, 145
inner judgment, 37–38
moral luck, 325
obligations, 145
promise-breaking, 100
utilitarianism (allowing
Hitler to drown), 424, 427

**Hobbes, Thomas
(Hobbesian):**
contractors, 556
equals, relationships
between, 726
ethical egoism and the
golden rule, 197
Foole, 556, 576–577
Leviathan (chapter 62), 558–570
moral agreements, 556
nature, 555
power, 173
state, origins of the, 555

utilitarian justification, 40
virtue and self-interest, 178
wants and demands, 30
holier than thou, 205
holiness:
eternity (and eternal
progress), 232
Euthyphro, 218–219
holy man, 700
Holy Wills, 517
moral law, 230, 232
Hollingdale, R. J., 580
Holocaust, 225, 281–282.
See also genocide
holy man, 700
Homer:
The gods themselves
can be swayed by
prayer, 135
When a good king, in
his piety, 135
homicide, 408, 630, 634, 640, 753
homo sapiens, 390, 393, 395, 397, 399
homosexuality, 227, 637
honor (honour):
arbitrator, 569
commitments and
perceptions, 746
common beliefs, 616
dead persons, 376
divine, 564
family, 36
good, the, 617
happiness, 485, 618
inclination to, 487
justice, 136
moral discourse, 742
non-person, 357

political life, 617
praise and, 620–621
reputation, 134
understanding, 629
vicious people, 135
virtue vs, 617
Hooker, Brad, 415
Rule-
Consequentialism
(chapter 50),
428–440
hope:
attitude, as an, 267
conative ability, 356
happiness, of, 233
human consciousness,
and, 703
object of, 232
passion, as a, 8
pious, 318
that others will do the
same, 39
truthfulness, for, 747
Hospers, John, 308, 311
Hottentots, 97
how the world is to be,
64
**Howard Roark
(fictitious
character),** 181
Hudson, Hoyt H., 509
**Hugh (fictitious
character),** 270,
275
human:
connection, 694
consciousness, 703
development, 226
physiology, 641
relationships, 344,
692, 696, 698
vegetable, 369, 377
humanism, 381, 385

**Hume, David
(Humean):**
active virtue, 699–700
agent-basing, 654, 656
constraint, 572
contractarian moral
theory, 727
error of reason, 4
ethical truth, 4
external objects, 29
final sentence, 699
gouty toes, 157
introduced, 3–4
justification of
induction, 352
knowledge, 28
logical and factual
disputes, 99
Moral Distinctions Not
Derived from
Reason (chapter 1)
, 9–15
moral duties, 62
nonmoral, 72
objectivism, 25
Of the Influencing
Motives of the Will
(chapter 1), 7–9
ought vs is, 4, 113
psychology, 64
reason, 29
self-interest, 714
skepticism & realism,
87, 94
sympathetic
identification, 572
Treatise, 5
virtue ethics, 647
virtue of justice, 721
humility, 112, 232,
634–635
humor, sense of, 201
hunches, 115, 117

hunger:
actions to relieve, 519
affecting others less,
199
bodily experience, 641
conceptual differences,
640
Formula of End in
Itself, 511–512
human universal, 636
invariant, 636
Kantians and, 512–519
moderation, 636
Treating Others as
Ends in Themselves
, 513
utilitarians and, 518
welfare and
dependence, 519
world, 511, 520
Hunt, Lester, 130–131
Flourishing Egoism
(chapter 20),
178–192
Hursthouse, Rosalind,
612, 678, 684
Normative Virtue
Ethics (chapter 68),
645–652
Virtue Theory and
Abortion
(publication), 664,
675
Hutcheson, Frances,
25, 656, 716
hypocrisy, 205, 510,
702, 710
hypotheses:
agent actions,
predicting, 60
black holes, 34
empirical, 16–17,
173–176
explanatory, 27

moral, 571
orchestrated beliefs,
87
prototype, 791
psychological, 176
scientific, 31, 34
skeptical, 87
synthetic propositions,
and, 16
thought experiments,
31
hysterectomy, 537, 541

I

I must, 699–703
ideal advisor, 6
ideal observer, 54
ideal speech situation,
579
idealization, 27, 150,
746
identity, law of, 174
good is good, 48, 52
pain is pain, 370
pleasure is pleasure,
51
idiot, 372–374, 377, 384
moral, 346–347, 678
savant, 678
im/piety, 135, 215,
318, 564, 584
**Ima Relativist
(fictitious
character),** 44–47
immoral conduct, 100,
149, 500, 508
immoralism, 443
immortality:
existence of, 216
lovers, and, 157
morally flawless, 216
soul, of the, 230–231
impaled, 134

impartiality:. *See also
partiality*
act utilitarianism, 414
calculations, 425
feminine moral
reasoning, 689–690
feminists, 691,
735–736
hypothetical
agreement, 579
insipid, 433
internalized, 433
interpretations of,
603, 788
intuitive standard, 577
moral point of view,
691
other-regarding, 149
overriding, 433
positive moral
interests, 207
principle of, 467
right of, 714
rule-consequentialism,
438
traditional moral
theory, 717
utilitarian, 414, 557
virtue ethics, 612
imperatives:
categorical, 24, 106,
108, 138–142,
148, 151, 206,
450, 481, 490–492,
494, 496, 499–500,
503, 505, 509–510,
523, 703
apriority of the, 106
duty, 493
hypothetical, 24,
138–140, 142–143,
490, 492, 496,
505–506, 509, 703
logic of, 40

moral/ity, 492, 697,
701
imperativist, 98
impersonality, 691, 735
implicit promise, 718,
757, 765
imputation, 258, 742
in foro externo, 569
in foro interno, 569
in the same boat, 63,
166, 749
incantations, 135
incest, 14, 227
income:
expenditure on
children, 186, 438
gender and, 715, 743
giving to the needy,
87, 439, 470
minimal, 518
re/distribution of, 517,
586–587
incommensurability,
107
inculcation, 5, 89, 792
incurable/s, 377, 383,
404, 629
indefinable, 17, 21,
49–52, 172–173
indeterminacy, 379,
671
India, 466–467, 472, 539
indirect applications,
532
**indiscernibility of
identicals,** 55
individual goals, 446,
696, 724
individualism, 574,
690, 724
induction/ inductive:
analogical and
narrative reasoning
, 744

citing cases, 239
deduction vs, 112,
    529–531, 591–592
deductive, abductive,
    explanatory, and,
    112
grounds for
    coherentism, 119
inductive
    generalizations,
    55, 177
inferential relation, 113
justification of, 352
moral presumptions,
    780
neighborhood guides,
    781
right and optimific,
    760–761
study of principles, 619
inept, 134, 495
inequality
inescapability:
bad faith, 93
commitment to acting,
    92
freedom, 314
God's existence, 226
grounding experience,
    636
interests and desires,
    139
moral reasons, 595
moral requirements,
    140, 164
morality, 140–141
responsibilities, 746
self-contradiction, 534
should, 140
thinking, 216
infanticide:. *See also*
    abortion;
    baby/babies;
    child/ren,

childhood
drowned baby, 325
mothers and, 704
objective wrong, 44
permissible, 398–399
right to life, 390
social utility, 402
inference:
accompaniment to
    purpose, 169
conclusions of, 55,
    103–104
counter-examples, 247
ethical disagreement,
    scope of, 56
FLO, 405–406
form validity, 102
general principle, 779
inductive, 530, 592
internal, 105
modes of, 98
moral judgments, 91
objectivism, 28
one or more premises,
    105
open and traditional
    societies, 684
pain in others, 365–366
passions, 559
reason, inadequacy of,
    10
reasons and, 164
responses (inference-
    based), 793
role of, 105
signs of contract, 562
special intuition, 28
valid form, 759
inferential (&
    non-inftl)
    knowledge, 101,
    103, 107

inferential/ evidential
    relations, 112–113,
    115, 118, 122
coherentism, 118, 122
epistemic credentials,
    122
epistemic priviledge,
    112
foundationalism,
    112–113
permissive justification
    , 115
information:
absence of, 590
false, 257
full, 162, 277–281,
    285, 287, 606
general, 588–589
impart (no)
    information, 174
information overload,
    383
information speck,
    703–704
misinformation, 590,
    716
missing, 697
nonmoral, 6, 56
particular, 588–589
propositionally
    represented, 104
ingratitude, 13, 567,
    569
inheritance, 374
initial impulse, 700
initial situation,
    582–586
initiations
    (indulgences), 136
injunction, 138, 523,
    697, 716, 787
injury:
avoiding, 540–541
non-, 102, 106

not injuring others,
764
injustice. *See justice*
rectification of, 102
innate, 81–82, 312,
341, 639, 701,
709–710, 792
inner circle/s, 702, 704
inner light, 223
inner strength,
656–659, 662, 669
innocence, 58, 202, 490
Inquisition, 227
instantiation, 648, 737
institution/s/al:
arrangements,
515–516
autonomous agents,
519
capital punishment,
404
claimant/ claimee, 372
community, 746
de facto social, 423
design, 724, 726
equal liberty, 586
ethical, 747
existing, 578
frames, 745
inequalities, 606
institutional loyalty,
448
judging, 785
justice, 588, 591
justifying, 583, 601
knowledge, 738, 740
mediating social, 153
monogamy, 97
moral philosophy, 739
moral psychology, 588
morality, 239
noninstitutional
affiliation, 711
policy, 736

practical deliberations,
511
private property, 239
promising, 423, 502
punishment and/or
reward, 316, 350
relations, 736, 741
requirements, 525, 532
sexism, 691
slavery, 41, 459–462,
640
social, 556, 578, 582,
721, 727
social unrest, 123
structured, 737
survival lottery, 476
underlying principles,
511
unjust, 36, 123
venues, 738
World Bank, 516
world hunger, 520
wrongness, 222
instrumentalism, 109,
166
insular circle, 448
integrity:
biotic community, 381
consequentialism, 415
demandingness, 415
deontological
requirement, 482
existence of, 191
experience, two
disparate modes of
, 698
indecent, 673
individual human life,
195
justice, 572
law, 497
moral, 187
moral decisions, 713,
742

Moral Luck, 720
moral practices, 307
moral understandings,
744
parties, of the, 746
personal, 719
physical, 532
resolutions, 746
women's sense of, 723
intellectual curiosity,
171, 344
intention/s:
act/s of will, 325
actions and, 456, 693
agent, 325
agreement in, 41–42
animals, towards, 370
attitudes and, 342–343
backfiring, 414
best of, 693
conscious, 733
consequentialists and,
683
culpability and,
324–325
deceive, to, 648, 778
determinism, 309
Difference Principle,
606
direct, 536–541
double effect, and, 484
evil/ immoral/ wicked,
164, 327
general, 263
God, 249
Golden Rule, 526,
533–534
good to oneself, of,
567
habits, dispositions, 39
harm, 546
intentional action, 176
intentional awareness,
636

intentional states, 155
intentionally bringing
    about, 315
intentionally doing,
    314, 341
intentionally
    performing or
    refraining, 696
laws, 240
maxims and, 511
oblique, 536–541
others', 342
parental, 171
power, those in, 464,
    628
promises and, 488,
    493, 501
selfish, 176
strength of purpose,
    659
upon the intention,
    422
utilitarians and, 660
wrongness, 221
interactions, history of,
    742
interest/s:
conflict of, 107, 541
nonmoral, 201, 747
objective, 222, 573
self-, 60, 129–131,
    139, 142, 159,
    161–163, 166–167,
    178–179, 181–183,
    188–192, 194–197,
    209, 239, 290,
    294, 296, 455,
    483, 487, 556,
    572, 601, 690,
    714, 717–719
special, 108
interior design, 202
intermediary, 588

**internal state of
    (im)balance,** 701
internalism, 125,
    144–145, 147–148,
    156, 160–161, 166
interpretation:
favored, 519, 584–585
general, 525,
    527–528, 530, 533
Logical Contradiction
    Interpretation, 504
normative moral,
    528–529
particular, 598
Practical Contradiction
    Interpretation, 508
interview, 168, 174,
    693–694, 697, 723,
    730
intramoral content,
    208
intrinsic:
Desert- Adjusted
    Intrinsic Attitudinal
    Hedonism (DAIAH),
    273–275
Double Desert-
    Adjusted Intrinsic
    Attitudinal
    Hedonism
    (DDAIAH), 275
good, 244–245, 255,
    257, 263, 286,
    299, 302, 387
Intrinsic Attitudinal
    Hedonism (IAH),
    269–271
intrinsic attitudinal
    pleasure, 269–270,
    272, 274–276
merit, 104
nature, 244–245, 247,
    768
value/s, 30, 53, 166,

244, 255–257,
    272, 275–276,
    413, 415, 447,
    453, 456, 482,
    613, 755
Veridical Intrinsic
    Attitudinal
    Hedonism (VIAH),
    271–272
worth, 53
intuit/ing, 72, 83, 770
**intuition/s (cf
    Anschauung,
    intuitus):.** *See also
    intuitionism*
apparent, 108
appeal to, 18
conflicting, 18
conflicting, 18
considered judgments
    and, 59
counterintuition, 78,
    189, 191, 437, 666
differences of, 6
faculty of, 28–29, 104,
    779
false, 108
idiosyncratic, 80
intellectual intuition,
    18, 231
moral, 6, 75–78, 397,
    436, 478, 651,
    738, 743
moral facts and, 6
moral sense/
    perception, as,
    27–29
prejudice
    masquerading as,
    108
reliability of, 79
widely-held, 79–80
intuitionism, 6, 28,
    72–73, 101–102.

See also intuition/s (cf Anschauung, intuitus)
conscientious, 108
moderate, 102, 109
out-and-out, 768, 770
particularist, 109
plausible, 108, 110
rationalist, 106
intuitive reactivity, 104
intuitively knowable, 101, 109
invariant, 636, 773, 778
inversion, 525–527, 531, 533–534
irrationality:
allegiance to morality, 236
basic rights, 483
immoral behaviour vs, 149
immorality of failure, 156
moral principles, 481
moral rules, 415
moral virtue, 238
should, ignoring the, 140
weakness of will, 63
irrealism, 65
irreducible plurality of moral principles, 102, 636

J

jail, 133, 196, 237, 334, 563, 694, 732
Jake (research respondent). *See Amy, Jake, Ned, Diane & Sharon (research respondents)*
James, William, 169
jargon, 280, 342
jealousy/envy, 259, 326, 461, 486, 491, 494, 560, 625, 642, 644, 657, 670, 721
Jesus, 417, 788
Jew/s:
Dialogue between a Philosopher, a Jew, and a Christian, 178
FLO and, 406
Hitler's order against, 37–38
identities and, 455
Lika Rebel and, 45
jewel, 322–323, 486
John (fictitious character), 684
John, Anne, Lisa, Helen (fictitious characters), 441–443
John, Mary and Valentino (fictitious characters), 790–791
Johnson (Dr) (fictitious character), 317
Johnson, Robert, 680
JoJo (fictitious character), 334–338
Jones (fictitious characters), 171, 396, 576, 710, 730
Jones and Smith (fictitious characters), 576
Jowett, Benjamin, 218
Joyce, Michael, 158
Juan and Linda (fictitious characters), 451
judgment (cf Urteil):
considered, 59, 404, 408, 573, 579, 585, 592
ethical, 16–17, 19–21, 54, 221
faculties, 260
false, 8, 12
inner (moral), 36–40, 42–43
intuitive (moral), 74, 743, 745
perceptual, 32
pre-reflective moral, 323
principle-based, 775
self-, 708
suspend, 57–58, 62, 71, 107
judgmental harmony, 601
Jupiter, 3, 564–565
jury, 359, 711
just, the most, 134
justice:
autonomy and, 714
care and, 566, 690, 714, 717, 727
circumstances of, 588
commutative, 566–567
conception of, 581–582, 584–589, 693, 696–697
convention/s and, 157
corruption of, 538
distributive, 458, 567
fairness and, 556, 581–584, 591
injustice, 10, 29, 32, 59, 110, 123, 129,

INDEX TO ETHICAL THEORY: AN ANTHOLOGY

132–137, 142,
374, 414–415,
513–514, 519,
560–561, 564–567,
569, 583, 587,
633, 697, 721
rectification of, 102
Justice, Care, and
Gender Bias
(chapter 74,
Calhoun, Cheshire),
713–720
love vs, 372
mercy seasoning, 721
orientation, 697
perspective, 722, 725
Plato and, 157, 657
procedural, 587
promoting, 668
reputation for, 132,
134
sense of, 364, 373,
573, 582, 585, 588
Theory of Justice, A
(Rawls, John,
chapter 64),
581–592
justificans, 526
justification:
a priori, 109
believing, for, 105
chain of, 73
deliberative, 573–575
dispositional, 105
epistemic, 112
indefeasible, 103, 108
intuitive, 104, 106
mode of, 573–574
moral, 72, 110, 364,
367, 573–574,
601, 691, 744
occurrent, 105
overdetermined, 106
permissive, 114–119,

123–124
positive, 57–58,
114–119, 124
practical, 574–575
prima facie, 159
process of, 101, 788
rational, 600
relativism about, 123
special, 75
structural, 105
unconditional, 117
universalistic, 575
utilitarian, 40

K

Kagan, Shelly, 72–73,
271, 276, 437
Nagel on the happy
businessman, and,
270
Thinking About Cases
(chapter 10), 74–84
**Kant, Immanuel/
Kantian:**
agent- neutrality
(analogy), 151
animals and, 355–356,
359–360
autonomy, 447
Christianity and, 572
deduction, 107
demons, 450
God and Immortality
as Postulates of
Pure Practical
Reason (chapter
26), 230–233
Groundwork of the
Metaphysics of
Morals (chapter 55)
, 485–498
imperatives, 24, 138,
481

Kant's Formula of
Universal Law
(chapter 56,
Korsgaard,
Christine), 499–509
moral epistemology,
106
moral precepts, 21
moral theory, 436
motivation, 38
neo-kantian, 151, 736
psychology and, 21
We Have No Duties to
Animals (chapter
42), 359–360
Karamazov's Thesis,
246–248, 251
karma, 240
Kaufmann, Walter, 580
Kay, Paul, 790
**Keating, Paul (former
Australian Prime
Minister),** 668
Keele, Cyril Arthur, 371
Kierkegaard, Søren,
709, 712
killing:
accidental killing of
children, 324–325
animals, of, 368–369
gratuitous, 388
innocent, the, 475,
477, 481, 770
intentional, 235, 481
letting die, and, 84,
474, 476, 539,
543–545, 547,
549, 551
negative, 477
pleasure and, 601
positive, 477
**King, Martin Luther,
Jr.,** 46

kingdom:
animal, 701
apple or a, 11
getting of a, 565
god, of, 232–233, 565
Gyges of Lydia, 133
Kingdom of Ends, 777
vegetable, 375
kleptomaniac,
320–321, 331–333
knowing the
difference
between, 95
knowledge (cf
Kenntnis, Wissen):
causal accounts of,
265
certain, 108, 379
conditions for, 107
external world, of, 96
good and/or evil, of,
94
grounds, 338
inferential, 101, 103,
107
know, 18
moral, 3–4, 28, 71–73,
95–96, 99, 101,
109, 112, 650–651,
675, 691, 715–716,
737, 739, 741,
744, 748, 755
nature of, 758
non-inferential, 101,
103, 107
nonmoral, 72
paradigm/s and, 381
practice vs, 24
self-, 230
theoretical, 713
theory of, 323
Kohlberg, Lawrence:
adolescence, 692
dilemmas, 693–695

Gilligan and, 722
interviewing, 693, 723
investigations
pioneered by, 786
justice, conception of,
693
Kantianism, 722
model, 708
moral education, 708
moral maturity, 693
moral maturity, 723
Piaget, Jean, and, 722
scale, 693
stages of moral
development, 693,
708, 723
women and, 695, 723
Korsgaard, Christine,
481
Kant's Formula of
Universal Law
(chapter 56),
499–509
Kramer, Richard, 711
Kraus, Oskar, 276
Kraut, Richard, 257
Cesire and the Human
Good (chapter 33),
286–293

L

La Rochefoucauld,
François de, 342
lab coat, 55
Ladd, John, 509
LaFollette, Hugh, 400,
428
Lamont, W. D., 373, 380
Lance, Mark, 784
language:
alienation (Marxist),
723
antique, 188

artificial, 103
common, 94–95, 261
consciousness, 367
consequences, 676
convention, 17–18
deontological, 442
evaluative, 778
foreign, 459
historical change, 455
inter-cultural ethical,
676
Kantian, 507
learning, 398
meaning in, 455
moral, 25, 30, 427,
695
phenomenalistic, 398
philosophy, 455, 633
rights, 725, 727
translation, 105
understanding, 105
law:
common, 792
criminal, 533, 542
divine, 30
giver, 226–227, 233
man-made, 693
natural, 43, 234, 305,
318, 321, 493,
500, 508, 725, 758
obedience to, 711
outlaw, 42
positive, 30
rule of, 306, 586
statistical, 317, 781
universal, 206, 233,
239, 481, 488–489,
493–495, 497,
499–501, 503,
505, 507, 509
violator, 524, 527, 533
Layman, Charles
Stephen, 217

God and the Moral Order (chapter 27), 234–241
Lazarus (Luke 16:24-26), 709
Le Lion d'Or, 203
leaking tap, 539
leaky boat, 539
learner, 132, 614, 681–685
learning:
  action, tendencies of, 420
  aspiration to improve, 681, 684
  cognitive improvement, 283
  desire-theory, 289
  developmental process, 613
  discursive skills, 744
  feelings, 744
  full-information theory, 278
  goal of, 681
  grammar, 641
  happiness, 620
  justifications, 601
  language, 398
  laws of nature, 569
  moral, 588, 613
  moral behaviour/conduct, 141, 788
  moral context/s, 96
  moral philosophy, 739
  moral vocabularies, 745
  pain, 641
  perception, skills of, 744
  process, 681
  right and wrong, 706
  rules, 433–434
  transfer, 699

v-rules, 648
virtue, 613, 681, 684
legal proceedings, 373–374
legislation (cf Gesetzgebung), 177, 231, 371, 373, 725
legislator, 30, 621, 629, 725
legitimacy, 16, 154, 159, 284
Leibniz, Gottfried Wilhelm, 55, 310, 359
Leningrad, 143
Leopold, Aldo, 381, 389
lesser evil, 226, 563
Levi, Edward, 223, 790, 794
lex naturalis, 560
lexical ordering:
  antitheories, of, 777
  duties, of, 768
  goods, of, 448
  principles, of, 591
lexicography, 48
liability, 259, 306, 325, 383, 427, 459, 587, 731, 735, 792
liberalism, 85, 93, 724
liberation, 361–362, 364, 371
libertarian/ism, 146, 351
liberty:
  advocates of, 519
  appealing to, 458
  Cold War, 519
  conscience, of, 586
  defined (Hobbes), 560
  demands of, 519
  deprivation of, 296, 558

divest oneself of, 561
equal, 581, 586, 591
equality, 519, 722
extensive basic, 586
favouring, 460
forgiveness, 563
individual, 458, 519
infractions of, 591
infringement of, (supposed), 458
interfering with, 146
just man, a, 142
limit, 555
love of, 259
misery, 560
moral ends, 142–143
others, for, 586
political, 586
principle of, 462
priority of, 591
right of nature (jus naturale), 560, 568
slavery and, 464
social values, 587
unrestricted, 519
welfare state, 519
licentiousness, 135
lies:
  fullfledged, 790
  prototypical, 790
life adjustment, 172
life and death, 186, 409, 438, 477, 510, 674
life insurance, 376
Lika Rebel (fictitious character), 45–46
Lincoln, Abraham, 170
linguistic fiat, 528
Lipsey, Mark, 389
Little, Margaret Olivia, 755

On Knowing the
"Why":
Particularism and
Moral Theory
(chapter 81),
776–784
livability, 379, 696
Locke, John, 28, 581,
591
logic/al:
boundaries, 373
canon, 530
capability, 96
inconsistency, 26, 99,
203
moral, 737
positivism, 28
logical constants, 174
long-term:
aim, 139
project, 139
Longino, Helen, 750
loser, 416, 555, 572,
604, 606
lottery, 115, 257, 408
survival lottery, 416,
474–478
**lOuverture, Toussaint
(l'Ouverture),** 461
love:
activity itself, 184
animals, 291
art, 374
children, 271
Euthyphro and the
gods, 215–219
excitement, 259
falling in love, 245
feelings of, 446
friends and lovers,
186, 188
God, 247
justice, 287, 619
life, 9

literature, 205, 290
loved ones, 131, 271,
414, 433
money, 261
morality, 203
music, 262, 290
mutual, 298, 302
neighbor (incl love thy
neighbor), 225,
417, 488
objects, 290–291
others, for, 157
painting, 290
pleasure, 172
power, 259, 290, 659
sake of, 442
self-love, 153–155,
195, 342, 493,
497–498, 503,
569, 670
something, 290–291
starving child, 72
tried, 446
truth and liberty, 142
virtue, 261–262, 619
wife, 182
worthy of, 233
Lovibond, Sabina, 747,
750
**Lowenberg/
Loewenberg, J.,**
177
loyalty:
city, to the, 143
institutional, 448
interdependence,
relations of, 736
motivation, 717
values, 745
virtue, 645, 652
Lucius, Garvin, 169, 177
luck:
circumstantial, 329
constitutive, 324, 326

moral, 166, 322–329,
667, 720, 759
Lukes, Steven, 644
luminosity, 103
Lunn, John H., 794
**Lutèce (NYC
restaurant, closed
in 2004),** 204
l'Ouverture, Toussaint,
461

M

Mabbott, J. D., 352
Macedonia, 459
machine/s:
activation of bodily
movement, 106
animals, children and,
332
confining animals to
machines, 292
desire and, 391
experience machine,
256, 264–275, 447
machine guns, 168
moral expertise and,
777
motility and, 394
perceptual machinery,
203
result, 265
rights and, 390
virtual reality, 116
MacIntyre, Alasdair C.,
571, 631
Mackie, John L., 4–5,
22, 62, 157, 571, 601
Subjectivity of Values,
The (chapter 3),
22–30
mad dog, 106
mad murderer, 539,
548

mad scientist, 86–87, 122

make & wont, 776

make sense, 314

making (bad-, good-, wrong-):
bad-making, 780, 782
good-making, 781, 783, 789
wrong-making, 357, 601, 672, 764–765, 780–781

malevolence, 170, 342

Malthusian/s, 516–517

Mandarins, 477

Māori, 676

market failure, 580

Marquis, Don, 357
Argument that Abortion is Wrong, An (chapter 47), 400–409

marriage:
arranged, 228
monogamy, 27, 97
polygamy, 97

martians, 395

Martineau, James, 654, 656, 659–660

martyrdom, 173, 175–176

Marx Brothers, 201

Marx, Groucho, 204

Marx, Karl (Marxian), 447, 461, 638, 643

Marxism, 222, 459, 644, 722–724

masochism, 659, 715

mass media, 736

materialism, 158, 312

mathematical axiom, 102, 760

mathematics, 67, 594–595

maximal(ly):
coherent, 119, 595
criticism, 277
fulfilling agent's preferences, 575–576
good, contribution to the, 452
good, promoting the, 437
happiness, 446–457, 516–517
moral theory, devotion to, 207–208
morally good, 209
morally worthy, 201
pleasurable, 429
preference fulfillment, 575–576
self-advantage, 454
sensibilities/ abilities, development of, 278
valuable course of action, 456

maximin (maximum minimorum):
principle, 589–591, 604–606
rule, 589–591
solution, 589

maximizing (maximising):
beauty, 413
behaviour, 575
choice, 575
coherence, 573
desire-fulfilment, 429
friend/ship, 429
good, 436, 668
happiness, 414, 416, 446, 515, 645
pleasure, 429
principle, 573

utility, 576
well-being, the sum of individual, 597

mayor, 547

McCormick, Neil, 794

McNaughton, David, 754–755
Unconnected Heap of Duties?, An (chapter 79), 763–771

meaning:
descriptive, 23, 28

means-end, 282, 284, 530

mediation, 12, 105–106, 109, 133, 442, 446, 497, 563, 568

mediis rebus, 573

meliorist assumption, 90

members of congress, 375

mental maturity, 102, 759

mercy:
Abraham and Lazarus, 709
demagogy, at the mercy of, 458
demands of, 777
existence of, 226
fate, 326
God, 564
moral virtue, 569
others, at the mercy of , 324
Portia (Shakespeare), 721

mere things, 375, 385–386

merit:

accepted standards, 29
actions, 11
artistic, 22, 666
conception of, 300–301
conformity to reason,
11
consequences, 325
contract, 562, 583
distribution of goods,
766–767
distribution of merit,
567
ethical, 178, 188, 190,
192
grace, 567
intrinsic, 104
justice, 754
justified disparaties,
525
killing, 566
meritum condigni,
562, 570
meritum congrui, 562,
570
moral standing, 382
objects, 12
pleasure and
happiness, 757,
764
reward, 754
self-interest and, 190
metaethics, 3, 54, 103,
147, 220–222, 382
**metamoral
assumption,** 210
metaphor:
compulsion, 321
event types, 321
generosity, 782
health and strength,
656
inner motives, 656
militaristic, 719
poetry as, 582

**metaphysical
necessity,** 28, 223
metaphysics:
(O) thesis from, 61
libertarianism, 351
metaphysician, in the
eye of the, 350
Metaphysics of Morals,
The (Kant,
Immanuel, 1797),
138, 143, 158,
485, 509, 591–592,
607, 712, 728
non-ethical concepts
and, 16
obscure, 379
metaprinciple, 92
Milgram, Elijah, 784
Mill, John Stuart, 90,
255, 413, 689
Hedonism (chapter 29)
, 258–265
Utilitarianism (chapter
48), 417–422
mind:
actions of the, 9–10,
12
emotion in, 9
kept in suspense, 8
laws and, 13
making up our, 3
operations of the, 10
perceptions and, 10,
14
qualities of our minds,
25
state of, 18, 53,
170–171, 185,
190, 256, 270–271,
294–295, 297,
301–302, 390–394,
398–399, 429, 442
will and the, 13
misanthropy, 160, 372,

780
misinformation, 590,
716
mnemonic, 788
modality, 55
model:
Aristotelian, 685
collaborative, 741
computational
(deductive), 791
computer manual, 680
deductive, 789, 793
developmental, 682
human, 375
husband, 441, 448
Kohlberg, Lawrence,
708
maternal, 690
prototype, 793
role, 207, 334,
681–682, 684
standard, 614
moderation, 135, 485,
632, 634, 658–659
modulo conguence,
699
money:
borrowing, 694
debt
non- payment of,
765
paying, 766
loan, 246, 249–250,
502, 505, 512–513,
694, 726
stolen, 239, 792
monism:
ethical intuitionism and
, 763
pluralism, 256
single rule/ value, 256
virtue ethics, 612
what makes right
actions right, 763

monkey and the coconuts, the, 699
monopoly, 46, 522
Moods (grammatical):
imperative mood, 24, 139
indicative mood, 26
optative mood, 26
Moore, George Edward:
attitudinal hedonism, 272–273
common language, 94
common sense, 94
conflicts of duties, 756
consequentialism, 763
cruelty, 271
Defense of Common Sense, A, 94
emphasis, 95
ethical statements, 20
good, 25
ideal utilitarianism, 757
individual actions, 423
inferential knowledge, 106
intuition/s/ ism, 110, 596
linguistic philosopher, and, 95
meeting Moore as an example, 267
moral propositions, 102
naturalism, 596
naturalistic fallacy, 50–52, 384
non-natural quality, 25, 28
open question, 210
organic unity, 125
perpetual indulgence, 272
Principia Ethica, 6
promise keeping, 102

Proof of an External World, 94–96, 98–99
right and optimific, 760
Subject Matter of Ethics, The (Chapter 7), 48–53
three ethical options, 6
Wittgenstein and, 94
worthless pleasures, 272
moral knower, 716
moral/s (cf Sitten, Sittlichkeit, Moral, Moralität):
absolutes, 226
action, 383–384, 413, 556, 711, 716–717
agreement, 35, 41–42, 556, 578
appraisal, 63, 306, 494, 597
argument, 63, 65, 67, 84, 96, 99–100, 227, 234, 240, 364, 595–599, 601–602, 605–606, 794
assessment, 86, 160, 164, 322–326, 413, 613, 742
attention, 381, 719
attitude, 20, 29–30, 326–328, 348–349, 351, 469
beings (i.e. not animals), 300–301, 755
beliefs, 27, 62, 64, 66–67, 72–73, 84–88, 90, 112–114, 123, 194, 307, 407, 416, 593, 595,

682, 716, 743, 771
blindness, 81
community, 349, 355–358, 380, 402, 556, 714, 742–743, 745–746
conflict, 649, 692, 695, 768, 770
resolving, 770
consciousness, 761, 787
considerability, 382–387
context, 25, 30, 95–96, 448. *See also non-moral*
deafness, 109
decision-making, 612–613
deliberation, 144, 387, 612, 689, 742
description, 777
determination, 326
development, 684, 690, 692–693, 695–696, 722, 728
stages of, 693
dilemmas, 650–651, 674, 693–694, 697, 723
disagreement, 6, 27, 46, 55–56, 62, 71, 81, 84–85, 88
discourse, 455, 695, 742, 747
dispute, 20, 41–42, 98–99
domain, 62, 78–79, 695, 698, 714, 728, 737
education, xvi, 20, 45, 149, 168, 172, 613, 629, 648, 676–677, 683,

699, 708, 711, 716
ends, 142, 163
enquiry, 98–99
epistemology, 6, 71, 73, 106, 112, 595, 691, 716, 735–736, 741, 744
equality, 363, 689
equation, 695
evaluation, 120, 160, 164, 166, 208, 384, 654–655, 660
experience/s, 16, 595, 600, 713, 718–719, 735, 739, 774
facts, 5–6, 32–34, 55–56, 59–67, 164–166, 216, 235, 283, 557, 574, 596–597, 600
faculty, 76, 787. *See also sense*
failure, 373
force, 602
habits, 21
heretics, 27
idiot, 346–347, 678
imagination, 749
imperative, 492, 697, 701
imperfection, 131, 777
import, 776–778, 780, 783
inertia, 546
issue of hurting, 695
judgments, 4–5, 18–19, 35–38, 40–43, 54, 85, 88–93, 106, 109–110, 113, 209, 306, 323, 325, 374, 408, 469, 482, 528, 573, 593, 692,

695, 697, 707, 715–717, 735, 739, 742–743, 745–746, 785, 787–792
judgments vs hypothetical judgments, 490
knower, 716
knowledge, 3–4, 28, 71–73, 94–96, 99, 101, 103, 105, 107, 109, 111–112, 650–651, 675, 691, 715–716, 737, 739, 741, 744, 748, 755
language, 25, 30, 427, 695
logic, 737
luck, 166, 322–329, 667, 720, 759
maturity, 693, 696, 723–724, 726–727
norms, 148–149, 152
conflict between, 692
objectivity of, 96, 98
opinion, 3, 32, 63, 97
orientation, 695, 713, 719
outlook, 88–92, 677, 722, 727. *See also contingency and controversy*
particularism, 435, 754, 775–776
perception, 705, 745
point of view, 91, 149–150, 194, 197, 209–210, 396, 435, 442–444, 467, 469, 535, 539, 583, 691, 782

practice, 63, 65–67, 107, 307, 441, 575–579, 775, 780
predicate, 60
premises, 99
presumptions, 780
principles, 20, 31–34, 41, 44, 47, 60, 82, 102–103, 106, 108, 110, 123, 142, 201, 381, 393, 395, 399, 463–464, 481, 583, 598, 603, 672, 696, 702, 710, 715–716, 763, 773, 785, 791
irreducible plurality of, 102, 636
progress, 97
proposition, 32, 98, 102–103, 691
psychology, 313, 330, 588
puzzlement, 702
questions, 63, 99, 456, 602, 663, 716, 755, 761, 770, 774
realism, xiv, 46, 54–57, 59–62, 65–67, 159, 166, 226–228
realm, 34, 226–227, 555, 755
reasoning, 99, 444, 463, 465, 510, 514–517, 593, 595, 598, 602, 685, 689, 708, 713, 719, 739, 744, 746, 786, 791, 793
record, 240, 326

reformers, 27
requirement, 5–6,
130–131, 140–141,
144–149, 151–153,
156–157, 163–164,
211, 216, 234–239,
241, 326, 378,
396, 415–416,
448, 511, 594,
600, 655
responsibility, 303,
305–316, 319,
325, 340–341,
349–350, 383,
421, 695, 735, 739
risk, 322
rules, 27, 47, 60, 140,
149, 197, 228,
374, 414–415,
421, 423–425,
427, 432, 434–435,
481–482, 555–556,
611–612, 639,
647, 649, 713,
736, 753–755
saints, 131, 200–211.
*See also
saintliness*
loving saint, 201,
203–205, 209
rational saint, 201,
203–204
sense, 20, 25, 27, 30,
72, 75–77, 80–82,
110, 347, 373,
528, 742. *See also
faculty*
silver lining, 778
skepticism (scepticism)
, 22–24, 26, 72, 91,
109, 455
specifically moral
element, 99
standing, 353,

355–358, 382,
406–407, 416, 556
terms, 23, 25–26, 44,
595, 737, 742–745,
747, 786
theory, 3, 21, 32–33,
74–79, 81, 87,
107, 113, 125–126,
145–148, 154,
156, 158, 199–200,
204, 207–211,
221, 238, 241,
363, 403, 416,
435–436, 441,
443, 447, 510–511,
572–573, 583,
596, 613, 654,
662, 675, 677–679,
682, 685, 690,
705, 713–722,
725–727, 735–739,
743, 761, 764,
770–771, 775–779,
781, 783, 786
thought, 5, 27, 29–30,
216, 510–511,
693, 717, 735,
737, 746, 748–749,
767, 786
turpitude, 14
upbringing, 682
view, 3, 5, 22, 32,
39–40, 42–43, 55,
57, 59, 63, 65, 96,
113, 123, 131,
196, 198, 248,
522, 579, 595,
652, 672, 707,
716, 747, 779
virtue, 16, 131, 142,
201–202, 207,
236, 238, 482,
611–612

**morality as
benevolence,**
662–663
morality/ moralities,
36, 200, 203, 453,
635
group, 42
rational authority of,
130
transmit, 788
unprincipled, 772–773,
775
morally fundamental,
766
**morally sensitive
promisor,** 376
Morgan, Kathryn, 737,
749
Morocco, 424–425
Morrison, Hugh, 190
mortality, 243, 637, 642
Mother Theresa, 207
mother/ mom/ mum:
breast-feeding, 725
caring, 699, 703–704,
708
child and, 690, 708
condition and
prospects, 662
death, 542
future existence, 662
infanticide and, 704
Ms. A (fictitious
character), 706
virtue, 674, 708
womb, 379
motility (im/motile),
393–394, 399
**motivation(al), motive
(cf
Bewegungsgrund,
Bestimmungsgrund):**
agents and, 20, 67,
160, 169–170,

176, 383, 386–387, 418
attitudes, 38
care and, 717
duties and, 159, 326, 418
efficacity, 572
overriding, 28
reach, 37
ulterior, 141–142, 238, 658
well motivated, 665–666
Mouw, Richard, 247, 251
movement:
anti-theory, 650
backward and, 749
feminist, 736
involuntary, 322, 327
learner to expert, 681
men's clothing, 731
natural laws, 758
nomads and pastoral people, 97
self-initiating sources of, 333
spontaneous, 393
Women's Movement, The (Didion, Joan, 1972), 698
Ms. A (fictitious character), 706
Ms. Poore, Mr. Gladwin, Ms. Goodwin (fictitious characters), 236–237
Munchausen/ Münchhausen, Baron (Raspe, Rudolf Erich), 315

Munich Agreement, 324–325
Murdoch, Iris, 777, 786, 794
Murphy, Jeffrie G., 592
Murphy, Mark, 248, 252
Musaeus, 135–137
Muses, 136
music (μουσική):
actions, 623
attachment to, 290
children, 289
full-information theory, 278
happiness, 171
intellectual curiosity, 171
just and temperate, 666
love, 262, 290
Plato's usage, 137
pleasure, 294
principle of utility, 261
remembering feelings, 706
virtuous act, 666
must, I, 699–703
mutual advantage/ benefit, 576, 582, 638
mutual consistency, 99, 517, 595
mutual disinterest, 556, 582, 606
mutualism, 526–527, 530, 533–534
mutuality:
rationally grounded, 532
mystery rites, 136
mythology, 41, 44, 46, 137, 725–727

N

Nagel, Thomas:
compatibilism, 306
Kagan on the happy businessman, and, 270
Moral Luck (chapter 39), 322–329
The Fragmentation of Value, 211
The Possibility of Altruism, 151, 158
namelessness, 379
Napoleon (Napoléon Bonaparte), 460–461
narrative of relationships, 694
Native Americans, 97
natural:
circle, 703
features/ properties, 25, 29, 110, 596
goods, 587
kinds, 790
object, 51, 324, 668, 759
properties, 29, 110, 596
science, 6, 61, 102, 761
naturalism:
definition of, 234–235
definitional, 596
epistemology, 455
law of nature, 560
naturalistic ethics, 6, 50–51
naturalistic fallacy, 50–52, 384
non-naturalism, 6, 25–26, 29, 54–55, 57, 59, 61, 596

reasonable/
unreasonable,
249
philosophical, 6
theist position vs, 236,
238, 246, 250
nature:
animal, 87, 260, 292,
359, 636, 733
human, 4, 13, 93,
124, 142, 158,
173, 176–177,
200, 258, 262,
282, 339, 347,
359, 417, 421,
433, 463–464,
494, 503, 642–644,
668, 675, 743
intrinsic, 244–245,
247, 768
man, of, 532,
558–559, 564
state of, 555–556, 581
Nazism/ Naziism:
compatibilism, 306
cultural relativism (CR)
, 45–46
death camps, 457
epistemic belief and
rejecting, 112
moral luck, 306, 323,
326
objective moral values,
and, 225
particularism and
dealing with Nazi
guards, 778, 782
responsibility, 336
sanity, 338
**necessary and
sufficient,** 20, 118,
389, 779, 790
**Ned (research
respondent),** 446

needs:
agent's/ our own,
193–194, 199,
338, 486, 525,
657, 710
balance of social, 440
citizens, of, 452
emotional, 723
human, 470, 490–491,
496, 635, 642
judges, of, 538
just people, of, 627
material, 517
needs of society, 469,
643, 657
needs of spouses,
441–442
nonsentient beings, of,
386–388
others, of, 83,
161–162, 194,
199, 362–363,
414, 515, 525,
658, 695, 717
parasites, of, 195
patients, of, 538, 544,
546, 549–550, 774
refugees, of, 466
unsatisfied, 488
women, and/of, 708,
715
negligence, 324–325,
569, 792
neuro- manipulator, 87
neurophysiology, 384
neutral capacity, 301
New World, 773
New Zealand, 670, 676
Newman, Paul, 202
Nicomachean Ethics,
153, 191, 615, 630,
632–633, 643, 675,
685
Nielsen, Kai, 245, 251,

749
**Nietzsche, Friedrich
(Nietzschean):**
agent-basing, 654
altruistic behaviour,
658
Basic Argument, 316
Beyond Good and Evil,
315, 658
causa sui, 315
death of God, 225
egoism, 658
health and strength,
656
moral philosophy, 207
morality, death of, 571
noble giving, 658
objective values
without God, 227
power, 711
psychological disaster,
595
revaluation of values,
674
sameness, 702
nihilism, 65, 227, 571
Nineteen Eighty-Four,
429, 711
2+2=4 (or 5), 175,
245
Nisbett, Richard E.,
793–794
Noddings, Nell, 690
Ethic of Caring, An
(chapter 73),
699–712
nomadic, 97
non sequitur, 89, 788
non- cognitivism,
25–26, 28, 65
**non-derivative
principles,** 55
core principles, 55

sources of moral duty, 754
non-hypothetical, 139–140, 142–143
non-inferential knowledge, 101, 103, 107
non-maleficence, 754, 764–765, 767–770
  vs beneficence, 757
non-performance, 107
non/ compliance, 5, 146–147, 431–432, 434, 438–439, 454, 456, 470, 576–579, 594, 670
noncontingent, 378, 387
noninferentially knowable, 109
nonmoral:
  fact, 4, 54
  goodness, 702
  interests, 201, 747
  practical judgment, 92
  reasons for acting, 204
  virtues, 201, 203–204, 208
nonrational/ism, 91, 352, 576, 621–622
  preferences, 576
nonsentient, 384, 386, 406–407, 580
nonviolence, 358, 698
normal course of events, the, 379
normalcy, 781
normative (normativity):.
  See also normative
  ethical symbols, 17, 19
  fact, 60–61
  question/ answer, 210, 281, 283

standard, 60–61, 741
theory, 103, 194, 277, 645, 650
norms:
  categorical (moral), 144, 146, 148–149, 151
  cultural, 631, 731
  etiquette, 148
  hypothetical, 149
  killing, against, 47, 469
  masculinity, 736
  property, 469
  rationality, 144–145
  societal, 44
  universal, 748
North American Free Trade Agreement (NAFTA), 662
North Americans, 313
northern hemisphere, 97
not-to-be- doneness, 28, 601–602. *See also to-be- doneness*
noumenal, 310, 714
Nowell-Smith, P. H., 351, 423
Nozick, Robert, 146, 152, 256, 275, 447, 455–457, 482, 521–523
  Experience Machine, The (chapter 30), 264–265
nuclear power, 203
Number One, looking out for, 690
Nussbaum, Martha, 612
  Non-Relative Virtues: An Aristotelian Approach (chapter 54

67), 630–644

O

Oakley, Justin, 673
objectivism/ objectivist, 6, 25–28, 95, 164, 180–181, 190, 429. *See also cognitivism*
  moral, 28, 164
  pleasure and, 429
objects:
  complex, 49
  external, 12–13
  external material, 94
  kinds of, 82–83
  material, 94, 302
  relations of, 7, 12, 14, 25. *See also relations and*
  theory of, 78
obligation (cf Verpflichtung):
  ascription of, 149
  care and, 700, 702
  conflicting, 110, 421
  Deity, on the, 10
  explanatory, 77
  fairness, 145
  final, 110
  general, 718
  moral, 30, 90, 130, 144–147, 154, 159–160, 163, 165, 197, 226, 246–252, 259, 309, 340, 421, 468, 717–718, 727
  morality, of, 14
  objectivity, 29
  obligated to do X,

702, 704
obligatoriness, 102,
    110, 761
organic, 110
other-regarding,
    146–147
others, to, 154, 194
overall, 110
perfect, 768
positive, 146
prima-facie, 38,
    390–391, 768
recognized, 582
special, 154, 713,
    718–719, 761
special, 154, 713,
    718–719, 761
values, 22
obtain universally, 531
**Occam's razor (cf
    William of
    Ockham),** 59
Oedipus Complex, 175
omnipotence, 56, 233,
    242–245, 248, 265
omnipresence, 233
omniscience, 216, 233,
    249, 265, 281, 491,
    665
one thought too many,
    206
one-caring, 700–711
one-size-fits-all, 682
ONeill, Onora (O'Neill),
    482
    Kantian Approaches to
        Some Famine
        Problems (chapter
        57), 510–520
ontology, 23, 55, 59–62,
    399
    ontological credibility,
        62

open question, 6, 210,
    582, 633, 643
    open moral question,
        377
operative agreement,
    106
opinion:
    common, 139
    considered, 757
    emphatic, 26
    fallible, 762
    general, 132
    human, 226
    moral, 3, 32, 63, 97
    observational, 32
    parochial, 5
    personal, 3
    probable, 759–760,
        771
    real, 765
    right, 301–302
    theoretical, 222
oppression, 45, 143,
    533, 722, 731–732,
    749
optimific, 424, 426–427,
    431, 439, 760–761
order:
    ends, of, 233
    first, 22–23, 27,
        102–103, 593, 595
    hierarchical, 189
    higher, 29, 107–108,
        745, 793
    lexical, 591, 768
    moral, 234–235, 237,
        239–241, 427,
        577–579, 759
    natural, 60, 470
    nature, of, 232
    nature, of, 232
    objectively purposive,
        575
    reality, of, 227

second, 22–23, 26–27,
    87, 103, 106–108,
    287, 331–333, 768
    serial, 586–587
    social, 20, 693
ordinary cases, 460
organ transplant, 31,
    39, 376, 474–475,
    477–478, 544, 549
    vivisection for, 416
organic arrangements,
    503
organic matter, 376
organic unity, 125
Original Position,
    581–591, 604–606
orphans, 356, 368
Orpheus, 136–137
**Orwell, George
    (Orwellian),** 210,
    429, 477–478, 711.
    *See also Nineteen
    Eighty-Four*
other(s):. *See also
    fellows, our*
    counting as, 527
    directed, 126, 572, 717
    interests of, 388
    plight of, 699
    present, 701
    regarding, 144–157,
        173, 657, 709
    self/selves, 153–155
ought (and ought not):
    believe, to, 60
    care, to, 142
    duty and, 14
    egoism and, 180
    emphatic, 142
    exist, to, 53
    expectation, 37
    good and, 30
    inclination vs, 87

inner judgment, 37–39
is and, 4, 113
judgment, 36, 39–40, 532
meaning, 19
moral, 36, 142
moral outlook and, 88
moral sense, 30
normative, 36–37
normative facts, 60
operator, as, 145
ought and ought not, 14
pain, pleasure, and, 177
psychological egoism, 167
rationality, 36–37
should and, 139–140
statements, 24
tell the truth, 19
to dance, 24
to do Y, 24
outerdirected, 172
over-ridable, 114
overpopulation, 696
overriding/ ness:
commitment, 444
disposition, 433
duties, 107, 717
impartiality, 433
invariably, 166
motive, 28
overridingness, 107, 239, 241
reason/s, 5, 107, 157, 217, 236, 238, 345
weight, 430

P

pacifism, 43, 91
pain and suffering, 368, 406

parable, 787
paradigm/s:
case of a feeling, 266–267
cases, 392, 783, 790–792
distinguishing cases and, 793
emendation vs, 783
finding appropriate, 792
intuitions and, 110
knowledge and, 381
mathematics as a, 98
maximin rule and, 590
moral motivations, 130
moral relationship, 690
moral standing (or lack), 357
morality, 437, 556–557
notions, 782
paradigmatically immoral, 130
paradigmatically right and wrong, 131
privileged valence, 782
self-evident propositions and, 101, 104
source of disagreement, 103
paradise ex congruo, 562
paradox(ical):
air of, 223–224, 449
claims, 175
deontology, of, 483
figure, 200
genuine, 149
implication, 93
subjectivism and emotivism, of, 98
Pareto efficiency (or Pareto optimality),

575
Parfit, Derek:
egoism, objection to, 179–180, 184
intrinsic value, 257
life well worth living, a , 268
Reasons and Persons (1984), 158, 190, 275–276
What Makes Someone's Life Go Best (chapter 34), 294–298
parochialism, 5, 56, 676, 680, 747
parricide, 13
parsimony, 59–60
parti-resultant, 758
partiality:
act utilitarianism, 414
contractors, 556, 718
ethnic groups, towards , 283
exclusivity, and/or, 748
false beliefs, 283
favoritism and, 572
friends and family, towards, 438
introduced into deliberations, 556
loved ones, towards, 414
morality curbs, 572
permissible, 439
self, towards, 438
veil of ignorance, 556
particular act/ ion:
act-consequentialism, 431
class of actions vs, 423
deliberation, 186
duty/ ies, 758, 760

general principles, 786
intuition, 83
mental attitude, 759
moral virtue, 131
particular
    interpretation, 525
pleasure/ desire, 170
promise- breaking/
    maleficence, 765
reason, in/conformity
    to, 566
rightness/ wrongness,
    759–760, 764–765
self-interest, 189
sexism, 730
systems/ frameworks,
    730
type t, action A, 20
particularism:
Aristotelian, 639
case by case, 435
general ideas about
    morality, 435
Intro to Part 13 Prima
    Facie Duties and
    Particularism
    (Shafer-Landau,
    Russ), 753–755
On Knowing the
    "Why":
    Particularism and
    Moral Theory
    (chapter 81, Little,
    Margaret), 776–784
reasons, holism of, 674
strong/ weak versions,
    672
unpredictability, 672
virtue ethics, 674
passing inclination,
    139
passion:
dominant, 202
false judgment, 12

fear, 564
instinctive, 373
reason vs passion, 7,
    12, 15
sport, 171
unjust actions, 566
victim of a senseless,
    288
**passivity of
    dependence,** 695
Passmore, John, 382,
    385
pastoral, 97
**patient in room 306,
    the (fictitious
    character),** 31, 33
Paton, Herbert James,
    503–504, 506, 509,
    534
patterns of behaviour,
    30
**Pavlov, Ivan
    (Pavlovian),** 464.
    *See also Skinner,
    Burrhus Frederic
    (Skinnerian)*
paying a penalty, 133,
    136
pedestrians, 323–324
people being things,
    327
perceptions:. *See also
    senses*
artistic, 419
beliefs controlled, 335
commitments and, 746
competing, 745
experience of desire,
    636
hypothesis, 27
impressions and ideas,
    10
mind, in the, 14

mind, present to the,
    10
moral, 745
moral equilibria, 743
narrative approach,
    746
objects before one,
    636
salience, 632
science, in, 108
sense-, 102, 761
senses, of the, 489
social positions, from
    different, 747
unfamiliar, 745
perceptual machinery,
    203
perceptual term, 790
perfect accordance,
    230
**perfection/ism (cf
    Vollkommenheit),**
    204, 209, 583
permission, giving, 539
Persian Empire, 97
person:
first, 149, 270, 656
third, 139–140, 149
personal ideals, 203,
    205, 208, 210–211
personal relationships,
    343, 345–346, 428
personality:
accidental handicap,
    327
endless progress, 230
gender differences,
    722
Kant/ ianism, 207, 326
moral, 208
moral agent, 207
public vs private, 205
relationships, 726
reprogramming, 391

INDEX TO ETHICAL THEORY: AN ANTHOLOGY

X's, 284
phenomenology, 61,
266, 374
philanthropy, 487, 760
**philosophy/
philosophical:**
ancient, 287
Aristotle and, 568
compatibilism and, 306
CR and, 46
education, of, 709
enjoyment and, 267
ethical, 16–17, 21,
195, 644
ethics and, 6, 54
ethics as, 54
European moral
philosophy, 24, 571
history of, 53, 58,
177, 293
language, of, 455, 633
mathematics, of,
593–595
medieval, 287
moral, 7, 11, 21, 24,
30, 76, 95, 138,
141, 177, 193,
196, 200, 204,
207–210, 251,
286, 342, 363,
409, 423, 435,
459, 489, 523,
542, 569, 575,
592–594, 679,
685, 690–691,
702, 735–736,
738–739, 744,
771, 785
modern, 143, 571
passion vs reason and,
7, 15
political, 163, 523, 555
psychology and, 737
reflection, 586, 719

speculative, 495
theory of knowledge
and, 323
Western, 215, 736
women and, 696
phobias, 279
phronesis (φρόνησις),
665, 779–780
**physical training
(γυμναστική),** 132,
137
physicalism, 61
physicists, 31, 55, 99
Piaget, Jean, 693,
722–723
pianists, 202, 614, 682,
684
Brendel, Alfred, 681
Picasso, Pablo, 206
piety (& impiety), 135,
215, 318, 564, 584
**Pindar (Ancient Greek
poet),** 136
pity (noun):
giving, 658
Nietzsche, 658
objective attitude, 344
pity, a (i.e. a shame),
350
self-, 710
self-pity, 710
virtue, 624, 674
Plato:
action-guiding and, 30
desire theory and, 290
egoism and, 192
ethical properties, 221
Euthyphro (chapter
23), 218–219
Glaucon, 129, 132,
134–137, 572
good, form of the,
654, 657

health and strength
and, 656
healthy soul and, 572,
657
Hobbes and, 555
Hume and, 572
Immoralist's
Challenge, The,
132–137
Immoralist's
Challenge, The
(chapter 15),
132–137
individual actions and,
656
justice and, 157, 657
mathematical
platonism, 594
moral philosophy and,
286
origins of morality and,
555
Plato (Dialogues)
Euthyphro, 30, 215,
218–219, 228
Gorgias, 157
Parmenides, 572
Phaedo, 246
Phaedrus, 158
Symposium, 158
platonic argument, 157
platonic asceticism,
634
Platonic Forms, 28–29
pleasure and, 623
principles and
arguments, 616
Republic, 129, 152,
572, 580, 657
self-interest and,
129–130
social contract theory
and, 555
soul virtues, 656

virtue ethics, 656
pleasant rituals, 135
pleasure:
abstinence from, 623
actions and, 17, 25,
   169–170, 172,
   184, 616, 758
aesthetic, 296
aims and, 145, 184
animals and, 259,
   300–301, 356,
   362, 367, 369, 384
benevolent, 170
brains and, 292
coldhearted people
   and, 285
conquest and, 559
deceived businessman
   and, 270–271
denying others, 550
desire and, 50, 167,
   169–172, 258–259,
   262, 428–429, 629
disinterest and, 569
disinterested
   benevolence and,
   169–170
distribution of, 757
Epicureans and, 258
ethical egoism and,
   194
feeling vs attitude of,
   266–268, 272
friendship/ sociability
   and, 629, 643
getting what one
   wants and, 168
gifts and, 387
giving oneself up to,
   493
giving others, 766
giving ourselves, 766
gluttony and, 189
god's/gods', 223, 244,

628
good and, 49–52,
   112, 300
good conscience and,
   168
goods of life (including
   future) and, 403
gratification and, 617,
   623
happiness and, 171,
   184, 258, 261,
   618–619, 627, 757
harming others and,
   757
harmless, 132
inferior, 260
intrinsic attitudinal,
   269–270, 272,
   274–276
intrinsic good and, 302
killing and, 601
laws and, 495
love of, 172
manipulation and, 429
material maxim and,
   141
meaning of, 51
mental over bodily,
   259
negative, 269
objectivism and, 429
objects and, 7, 11,
   272–273, 276,
   302, 619
pain and, 7–8, 11,
   168, 258–263,
   268, 270, 273,
   275, 294, 299–301,
   356, 362, 367,
   369, 375, 381,
   385, 428, 623–626,
   629, 641, 661
peace of mind and,
   428–429

physical and mental,
   281
physical sensation and,
   173
plants and, 375
pleasant sensations
   and, 173
pleased (adjective)
   and, 51
pleasure is the (only)
   good, 48, 53
power and, 559
ranking of, 256
reason and, 9
revenge and, 9
rightness and, 301
sadistic, 73, 105, 110,
   121, 166, 271,
   296–297, 415, 778
satisfaction
   (gratification) and,
   172–173
sensory, 172, 222,
   268–270, 301, 384
sensual, 564, 659
sentiments of, 14
sexual, 523, 528
slaves and, 460
sponteneity and, 443
supremacy of, 621
undeserved, 301
utilitarians/ism and,
   428, 447, 758
value and, 255–257,
   262, 281, 298
virtue and, 255–256,
   262, 299, 301,
   619, 623, 632,
   642, 667–668
Wohl, das, and, 300
worthless, 271–272
wrongness and, 222

pleonectically, acting
(πλεονεκτέω/
πλεονεκτειν), 137
pluralism:
consequentialism, 661
cultural, 612
deontic, 763
good, the, 292
monism, 256
Moral Knowledge and
Ethical Pluralism
(chapter 13, Audi,
Robert), 101–111
newcomer to
philosophy, 292
value, 256–257
virtue ethics, 652
poetry:
justice/ injustice and,
136
metaphor and, 582
paradox of hedonism,
and, 171
Pindar (poet), 136
pushpin and, 255
young people writing,
705
μουσική, 137
Polemarchus
(Πολέμαρχος), 137
Polynesians, 97
Porky (fictitious
character), 272–273
porous, 781, 783
portions of the world,
327
position to help, in a,
694
possible world/
universe:
ethical truths and, 246
evil of suffering in, 245
happiest, 516
loving God, 223–224

metaphysical necessity
, 223
moral agents and, 759
properties, 224
truth claims, 245
postconventional,
696–697, 723
posterity, 379, 589
posthumous
arrangements, 376
power:
absolute, 464
accomplishing
purpose/s, 322
accounting for, 28
active, 310
analysis of, 306
animals, unborn
and/or future
generations, 372,
378, 727
avoid, to, 317
bad men, 539
benevolence, 655
causal, 59–62
choice, of, 320, 695
Chomsky on, 477
civil, 564–565
coercive, 563, 565
common, 559–560,
562, 565
communication, 503
conquest, 559
constructive, 637
contract, 562
defining cases, 49
discrepancies, 556
discretionary, 743
doctor/s, 475, 477
duty, 711
emotional, 186
endangerment, 559
epistemological, 736
equal lack, 329

events, of, 321
focus of, 461
for its own sake, 290
generalizations,
adducing, and, 783
God, 216, 222, 233,
242–248, 564
god-given, 135–136
habit, of, 263
happiness, 171,
231–232, 261,
418, 485
human character, over
, 417
imperative/s, 491
in/justice, 132–133,
136
inequality of, 564,
715, 726–727,
736, 738
influencing, 29
interests, 715
intrinsic goodness, 291
inverting, 137
liberty, 560
logic, of, 693
Longino, H. on, 750
love of, 259, 290, 659
marriage, in, 743
minimal, 109
moral development,
722
moral relationships,
726
moral strength/s, 202
motility, 394
Nietzsche on, 711
nuclear, 203
omnipotence, 244
others, over, 57, 290,
461, 464
perception, 28
perfect, 215
pleasure and, 559

political, 129, 620,
736–737
power- sensitive
conversation, 740
preventing bad,
467–468
priviledge, 739
purchasing, 518
reason, 109
regimes, 323, 461
sanity, 334–335
Sardanapallus, 617
seeking, 290
self-regarding motive/s
, 173
selfishness, 170
single, 558, 565
slavery and, 464
social power structures
, 715–716, 719, 739
societal, 724
source, 333
sovereign, 566
spirits, 564
statistics, 193
theoretical, 630
Third World, in the,
515
those in, 464, 628
transparency, 747
types, 135, 335
virtue, 262, 628, 655,
695
Western society, 747
practical skill, 490, 681
pragmatism, 105, 112,
205, 444
preaching, 177, 471
precedent, 568, 794
preference fulfillment,
576
pregnancy, 400–401,
695

premise/s:
cogent, 102
explicit, 104
false, 406, 590, 605
major, 402
minor, 791
rejecting, 236
theoretical, 106
premoral:
good, 702
reflective capacity, 578
situation, 577
prenatal injuries, 378
prescriptivism, 221,
594
presidents, 163, 406,
545–546, 548, 581,
662
preventable evil, 468
previous acts:
one's own, 764
other's, 764
Price, Richard, 25, 28
**Prichard, Harold
Arthur,** 106, 763,
791
pride, 91, 181, 259,
315, 327–328, 374,
564, 569
**principle/s (cf
Grundsatz,
Prinzip):**
core, 55
determining, 231–232
difference, 605–607
first, 260, 421, 497,
586
general, 27, 82, 141,
199, 301, 403,
503, 525, 527,
643, 755, 758–760,
764, 771, 779,
786–788, 792

hierarchical ordering of
, 697
interest, 375–378,
385–387
maximizing, 573
metaprinciple, 92
moral symmetry, 396
non-derivative, 55
practical principle
apodictically, 490
assertorically, 490
material, 141
problematically, 490
Principle of Generic
Consistency (PGC),
529–533
Principle of Humanity,
482
principle of utility,
120, 260–263,
420–421, 582,
611, 689
underived, 767
underlying, 511
universal, 495, 630,
708, 792
universalizability, 27,
481–482, 534, 689
prison. *See jail*
privacy, 194
private individuals,
135, 372, 538
privileging move,
781–782
probability:
being anyone, of,
603–604
calculations, 590–591
child drowning, 438
extreme utilitarian, 424
giving vs government
assistance, 471
good or evil, bringing
about, 759

increased response, 703

Influencing Motives of the Will (Hume), 7

probable outcomes, 538

seafarer's calculations, 425

theism, of, 234

working out the, 424

problem-solving:

descriptive, 789

factual, 790

normative, 789

procedure:

decision, 430–432, 435, 450, 613, 651, 664, 677–679, 681–685

rule-governed, 791

unitary justificatory, 767

process:

developmental, 613, 681

inferential, 793

learning, of, 681

mental, 186, 793–794

productiveness, 181, 761

progress in infinitum, 232

project:

acceptance of, 141

Anglo- French Concorde, 466

antitheorist, 776

Aristotelian, 637

codelike theory, 738–739

common, 139

compatibilist, 306

completion of, 92

deception, of, 512

development, 514

end, as an, 444

feminism, 729, 736

foundationalism, 573

ground, 446–447

Groundwork in, 500

hedonistic life, 444

human good, multiplicity of, 293

justifying norms, 631

Kant's, 500–501

knocking down icicles, 288

life, 444

long-term, 139

moral considerability, 389

moral realism, 62

pluralistic, 293

undesirable restrictions, 139

Virtues, 676

promises:

breaking, 437, 532, 745, 765

keeping, 95, 100–103, 108, 196–197, 301, 414, 423, 502, 576, 612, 647, 649, 658, 757, 761, 769–770

promissory note, 77

promote happiness, 447

proof:

Bambrough, Renford (chapter 12), 94–100

burden of, 163, 179–180, 574

defective, 103

external world, of an, 94–99

God's existence, of, 216

good character, of, 419

in/capable of, 110, 260

need no proof (proof-exempt), 102, 759

negligence, of, 792

principle of utility, of, 262

Pythagoras's theorem, of, 99

proper names, 375

property (characteristic/ Eigenschaft):

beliefs, of, 118

checklist theory, 790

common, 221

contrary to the commands of a loving God, 222–223

epistemically justified, 61

fetuses, of, 403

fittingness, 596

higher order, 29

moral suitability, 596

objective moral, 57

pleasure, 301

sensations, 172

unique, 53

wrongness, 222–224

property (possession/ Besitz):

animals as, 464

division and appropriation of, 470

God's, 247

meddling with others', 420

owner, 247

private, 97, 239, 643
right to/of, 378, 394, 458
taking others', 469, 496
prophets, 135–136, 190, 725
proposition/s:
analytic, 53, 491
articulated, 790
epistemic status of, 61
first-order, 103
genuine, 19
propositional object, 102
second-order, 103
self-evident, 101, 103–105, 109
synthetic, 16, 18, 491
theoretical, 230
protons, 33
prototype/ prototypicality:
effects, 790
hypothesis, 791
schema, 790
semantics, 790
proxy/ies, 374, 376–379
prudence:
acts, 236
analogy with, 151
choice of means, 490–491
circumstances altering cases, 97
counsels of, 491
definition, 490, 497
elementary, 372
environmental protection, 372
experience, 420, 558
imperatives of, 491–492
maxim of, 489

mind faculties, 558
morality vs, 237–238, 576
motives, 659
private, 497
rules, 138
temporal dissociation, 151
virtue, 619, 622
wellbeing, 490
world knowledge, 497
Prussians, 460
pseudo-concepts, 18, 21
psychoanalysis, 642
psychology/ psychological:
a priori, 318
abnormality, 338, 345
attributes, 402
autobiography, 652
breakdown, 281
cognitive, 790–791, 793
continuity, 153–155
deep structures, 708
disaster, 595
egoism, 130, 167–168, 173, 175–176, 194
fact, 167, 261–263, 787
hedonism, 172–173
hypothesis, 176
meanness, constituents of, 29
normal people, 278
physiology, and, 281
relationships, logic of, 697
social, 685
theories, 726–727
public domain, 702
public office, 135
public policy, 518, 606,

792
publicity, 450, 456, 467, 515, 583
pull out of thin air, 677
pumpkin/ princess story, 377
punching, 543–544, 551
punishment:
animal cruelty, 706
blameworthiness, 160–161, 340
children, 168, 348
covenant, 565
Decembrists, 324
demon, by, 450
determinism, 309
deterrent, 464
duty of justice, 766
fitting, 316
gods/ God, by, 136, 228–229
Golden Rule, 525
hell, 314
initiations, 136
institution, 350
intuitionism, 766
Kant, 450, 483, 525
moral condemnation, 340–342, 349–350
moral responsibility, 309, 315
murder, for, 407
necessary postulate, 216
one-caring, 706
rational, 426
rehabilitation, 350
revenge, 9, 567
reward and, 24, 168, 172, 216, 309, 315–316, 766
self-, 287, 290
self-accusation, 564
slavery, 461, 464–465

utilitarianism, 521
wrongdoer already
    suffered enough,
    766
younger victims, 407
Φ-ing, for not, 160
pure aesthete, 203
purpose:
actual purpose, 138,
    575
possible purpose, 490,
    493
Putnam, Hilary, 639,
    790
Pythagoras's theorem,
    99

Q

Quaker, 223
quantum mechanics,
    781
**quarrel, principal
    causes of,** 559
quarreler, 526, 533
queen/s (royalty),
    668–669, 725
queerness, 5, 26,
    28–29, 65, 67, 309
question(-) begging,
    57–58, 87, 164, 204,
    234, 238, 245, 310,
    357, 402, 450, 476,
    732, 767, 774
quickening, 399

R

rabbi, 788
races:
black (race), 199,
    362–365, 393,
    461, 733

white (race), 199,
    362–363, 393,
    406, 461, 733
Rachels, James, 131,
    551
Ethical Egoism
    (chapter 21),
    193–199
racism/ ist:
actions, 45
arbitrary, 199, 369,
    406
differences, 199, 715
grounds for, 199
groups, 198
Jefferson, Thomas, on,
    364
justice, 721
majority, 45
motivation, 669
objective moral views,
    227
principle of equality,
    365
relativism, 6, 45–46
speciesism/ sexism,
    362–363
superiority, 362
test case, 45
traits, 691
Truth, Sojourner, on,
    364
virtuous agent, 673
radical rethink, 690
radiologists, 791
Railton, Peter,
    184–185, 415
Alienation,
    Consequentialism,
    and the Demands
    of Morality (chapter
    51), 441–457
Rand, Ayn (Randian):
altruism, 196

Atlas Shugged, 180
Branden, Barbara, and
    , 196
egoism, 179, 182–183
Fountainhead, The,
    181
friends and, 187–188
sacrifice, 189
self-interest, 181–182,
    189
value and virtue,
    181–182
**Raphael, David
    Daiches,** 535, 763
**Rashdall, Hastings
    (Rashdallian),** 756,
    787, 794
rather than doing, 648
rational:
action, 109, 150, 277
beings, 10, 24, 151,
    230–233, 383–384,
    454, 488, 490,
    493–498, 500–501,
    503–504, 509,
    513, 777
choice, 120, 126, 292,
    571, 583–584,
    603, 605–606
condition, 233, 585
criticism, 64–66, 631
decision, 361
reconstruction, 576
reflection, 579, 581,
    716
will/ing (voluntas),
    500–501, 509,
    528, 723, 727
**rational- desire-
    transfers,** 531
rationalism:
antirationalist
    argument, 161
antirationalists,

164–165
Clarke, Samuel, 24
Kantian, 148
moral, 62, 159–161,
163–166
strong/ weak
rationalist theses,
156–157
rationality:
autonomy and,
355–356, 482, 514
Concept of Rationality
(COR), 282–285
deliberative, 575
irrationality. *See*
irrationality
objectivity and, 99
Rawls, John
(Rawlsian):
burdens of judgment,
85
contractarianism, 556
counting blades of
grass, on, 296–297
influence of experience
, 90
Original Position,
581–582, 584–591,
604–606
perspective of eternity,
443
purity of heart, 454
Rawlsian test, 579
Theory of Justice, A
(chapter 64),
581–592
Two Concepts of Rules
, 502
reactive attitude, 307,
343–350, 742
Reader, Soran, 674–675
realistically construe,
59–62

reason (good sense)
(cf Vernunft):
man of, 690
reasonableness, 528,
598, 604, 733
reason, faculty of (or
discourse) (cf
Verstand), 4, 364
reason/s:
action, for, 5–6, 38,
62, 65, 130,
144–145, 147–148,
150–152, 156–157,
159, 161–163,
165, 179, 772
giving, 5–6, 140,
163–166, 778
practical, 91–93, 106,
108, 141, 143,
148, 166, 201,
206, 230–233,
497, 499, 503,
505, 509, 631, 739
pure practical, 206,
230–233, 739
sufficient, 367, 509,
529, 531–532
reasoning, 786, 793
circular, 14, 73, 99
mode of, 98
parity of, 59, 95
practical, 143, 443,
503, 743, 788
security of, 98
reasoning-that, 791
reasons (causes):. *See*
also cause (cf
Ursache) causality
for acting, 37, 92,
140–141, 143,
204, 425, 444, 529
rebut vs refute, 110

reciprocity:
benefit, 599–600
caring, 703
cooperation in sin, 524
desires, 528
fairness (agents/
recipients), 534
feminism, 736
formal logic, 697
Kohlberg's stages, 693
love, 344
moral constraints, 454
mutual respect, 737,
743
noninterference, 723
right, 561
rule-, 525–527
unselfconscious, 704
utility, principle of, 582
recognition:
facial, 791
pattern, 791
public, 588
rectification, 102
reduction, 17, 439,
519, 605, 731, 758
reductionism, 788
reductionist, 788
refection, 102
referee, 588–589
reflection/ reflective:
capacity, 578
conclusions of,
103–104
conscious, 80, 184
equilibrium, 150, 273,
436, 573, 579,
585, 743, 745, 750
mediation of, 105
non-reflective
cognitive capacity,
104
refugee, 466–468,
471–472

refute vs rebut, 110
regress:
    argument, 73,
        114–116, 119, 123
    causa sui, 315
    deliberation/
        time-allocation, 449
    infinite, 73, 114, 173,
        691, 748–749
    problem, 72
    stopping, 114, 117,
        123
Reid, Thomas, 310
reiterative, 695
relativism (moral), 5,
    35–47, 123, 145,
    156, 158, 165, 612,
    631, 635, 637, 639,
    674, 702, 707
relativity, 26–27, 38,
    47, 66–67, 97,
    156–157, 598, 634
    considerations, to, 38
**reliably or
    characteristically,**
    680
religion:
    Buddhism, 85, 90
    Christian Science, 96,
        774
    Christian/ity, 30, 38,
        67, 96, 173, 178,
        190, 220, 222–223,
        225, 229, 232,
        246, 251, 258,
        290, 313, 419–420,
        517, 579, 634–635,
        641, 699, 725, 774
    Kant, Immanuel,
        572
    love, 699
    Hinduism, 240–241
    philosophy of, 251

    Roman Catholicism,
        223
religious intolerance,
    585
reparation, 102, 754,
    757, 764, 767
repentance, 567, 758
reproductive capacity,
    695, 729
reputation:
    charity, 142, 561
    generosity, 660
    good and desire theory
        , 290
    injustice, 129, 134,
        137
    justice, 132, 134–137
    lying, and, 196
    motives and, 511, 576
    pleasure and, 172
    posthumous reputation
        , 376–377
    quarrel, causes of, 559
    should, and, 140
    true and false, 137
requirement:
    basing, 122, 126
    conduct, 531
    evidential consistency,
        125
    explanatory, 122
    moral, 5–6, 130–131,
        140–141, 144–149,
        151–153, 156–157,
        163–164, 211,
        216, 234–239,
        241, 326, 378,
        396, 415–416,
        448, 511, 594,
        600, 655
    self- consciousness,
        390, 398
    utility, 419

resentment:
    beneficence, 669
    egalitarian propensities
        , 674
    Freedom and
        Resentment
        (chapter 41,
        Strawson, Peter),
        340–352
    gratitude and, 342–344
    instincts, 9
    Martineau's hierarchy
        of motives, 659
respect for human life,
    145, 478, 517
**respect for the moral
    law,** 141, 206
responsibility/ ies:
    agent, 330–335, 338,
        343, 421
    animals and, 309–311,
        332–333
    care and, 330, 695,
        697–698, 724
    care, for, 695
    choice and, 695
    definition, 309, 742
    determinism and,
        305–308, 319
    domain of, 325
    moral, 303, 305–316,
        319, 325, 340–341,
        349–350, 383,
        421, 695, 735, 739
    Nazism, 336
    rights and, 697
restraint, 85, 147, 575,
    786
result:
    background/
        experience, of, 90,
        115
    conscious reflection, of
        , 80

counter(-) intuitive, 285, 666
cultural conditioning, of, 227
desired, 232, 272–273, 589
fair agreement, of, 582
false beliefs, of, 283
formula, of a, 684
future, 183
good, 255, 413–416, 657
good fortune, of, 270
habit, of, 263
machine, 265
practical, 199
resulting judgment, 39
resulting theory, 40, 112–113, 273
resulting value, 275
sound, 110
test, 31
unconditional a priori law, of an, 230
voluntary action, of, 536
wisdom, of, 185
revelation, 223, 419, 563
revenge, 86, 91, 133, 508, 538, 559, 567
Revolution, 323–325, 508, 690
Revolutionists, 534
rhyme or reason, 310
riches/wealth:
accumulation of, 446
beneficiaries and, 376
desire for, 555
desire theory and, 290
duties of mutual aid and, 147
equitable (and inequitable)

distribution, 452, 583
famine relief and, 470
force and, 134
good will and, 485
good, the, and, 290
homelessness and, 518
injust and, 135–136
interests and, 582
just, being, and, 129
motives and, 290
non-moral goods and, 528
outdoing enemies and, 134
poverty-amid-wealth, 518
self-interest and, 129
riff, 782
right of nature (jus naturale), 560
right/s (cf Recht/droit):
basic, 483, 581–582, 586
born, to be, 378–379
claim, 531–532
correlative, 376
dead, of the, 376
doing the right thing, 186, 654, 676–677, 679, 681–683, 685
duties and, 581
equal, 536
generic, 529–534
getting it right, 612
holder, 356, 375, 385
human, 47, 386, 458, 510, 513, 518–519
life, to, 357, 369–370, 375, 390–402, 406–407, 409, 475, 542

might does not make, 228
moral considerability and, 382–387
natural, 364, 470, 560
negative, 540
not right not to give, 694
optimific and, 760–761
positive, 540
possessors of, 377
property, to, 378, 394
proprietary, 507
responsibilities and, 697
right (definition), 683
right opinion, 301
sue, to, 378
thing-rights, 374
virtue ethical criterion of, 664
vote, to, 361–362, 406, 586
rigorist, 91, 683
Ring of Gyges, 133, 157. *See also Republic*
risk:
avalanche, 548
aversion to, 587
collapse, 432
divergent answers, 210
famine, 510–512, 515, 518
good, the, risk of error in, 49
lives for others (Kant), 518
lottery scheme, 476
moral, 322, 759
rule violations, 555–556
Russian bomb, 548
saving a child, 438

starvation, ending, 470
trolley problem, 547
ritual, 40–42, 135–136
Robin Hood, 474
robot, 309, 365–366
robust animal realism,
87
rocks:
moral standing, 357,
372–373, 375, 386
strata, 60
throwing at ducks, 288
role model, 207, 334,
681–682, 684
Rome, Ancient, 44
root conception, 453,
457
Rorty, Amelie E., 210,
339, 777, 784
Rosati, Connic,
280–281, 284
Ross, W. D. (Rossian):
conclusions, 103
consequentialism,
436–437, 753, 767
critics, 764
DAIAH, 274
derivation, relation of,
765
derivative duties, 766
final list, 767
fittingness, 596
goodness vs rightness,
664, 666
hedonism, 257, 273
intuitionism, 102–103,
763–764, 768
knowing inferentially,
106
lying, 753–754, 765
mathematical
platonism, 594
moral judgment,
770–771

moral theory, 770
original list, 764, 767
preventing misery for
others, 753
prima facie duties,
102, 108–109,
546, 702, 751,
754, 757–758,
760–761, 764–766,
768, 770
process of moral
reasoning, 791
ranking moral duties,
768
ultimate values, 257
unconnected heap of
duties, 754
universal beneficence,
766
What Makes Right Acts
Right? (chapter 78)
, 756–762
What Things are
Good? (chapter 35)
, 299–302
what we really think,
108
Rostov, Natasha, 202
roué, 524, 526, 533
roulette, 310–311, 546
Rousseau,
Jean-Jacques, 447,
556, 581, 591
rule/s:
club, 139–140, 143
duty, of, 139, 418
everyday (ethical), 677
following, 789
game, of the, 381, 693
governed, 674,
790–791
guided, 779
ignoring, for, 789
legal, 372

prudence, of, 138
social, 47, 413–415,
524, 527, 532–533
thumb, of, 423–425,
427, 590, 755, 780
Ruse, Michael, 225
Russell, Bertrand, 26,
225, 229

S

sacrifice:
behalf of another, on,
154
compensation for, 151
definition, 189
diachronic,
intrapersonal
compensation and,
151–153
for its own good, 146,
523
future benefit, for, 155
greater benefit, for,
146
innocent bystander, of,
31
one's own interests,
170
self-, 171, 226, 432,
437, 660, 695–696
ultimate, 131, 476
sadism, 73, 121,
296–297, 338, 525,
678, 754, 778
sailors, monkey and
coconuts problem,
699
saintliness, 476
sake, 375, 385
salience/ nt:
analyses of, 740
because, 789
care, ethics of, 716

cases, 83
COR, cognitive
    perspectives in, 283
disagreement on, 669
druggist, lying to, 694
evils, two, 722
heuristics, 780
laughing animal, 642
morally, 636
non-compliance
    problems, 434
patterns of, 790, 794
perceptions, 632
philosophical history,
    feature of, 58
rights, 373
sex, Greek thought on,
    636
sexism, 730
virtue, 671
Salmond, John W.,
    540, 542
salvation, 241
Samaritan, 787
sameness, 702
sanatorium, 377
**sanity (and insanity
    and madness):.**
    See also mad dog;
    mad murderer;
    mad scientist
cognitive overload, 281
freedom, 341
madmen, 372, 377
responsibility, 330
Sanity and the
    Metaphysics of
    Responsibility
    (chapter 40, Wolf,
    Susan), 330–339
**Sardanapallus/
    Sardanapalus,** 617

satisfaction:
balance of, 582
desires, of, 145
guarantee of, 169
satisfaction thesis, 173
**Sayre-McCord,
    Geoffrey,** 6, 73
Coherentism and the
    Justification of
    Moral Beliefs
    (chapter 14),
    112–126
**Scanlon, T.M.
    (Scanlonian),**
    556–557
Contractualism and
    Utilitarianism
    (chapter 65),
    593–608
schema, 164, 348, 680,
    682–683, 685
cognitive, 790
prototypical, 790
schizophrenia, 377
**Schweitzer, Albert
    (Schweitzerian),**
    387
scientific acceptance,
    107
scientific method, 280,
    677
scruples, 134, 503
season/s:
autumn, 171
spring, 171, 618
winter, 171, 236, 288
seeing-that, 791
seem to say more, 25
self and other,
    695–697, 710, 777
self- improvement,
    102, 757, 764,
    767–768

self- righteousness,
    702
self-assessment, 332
self-conception, 357,
    574–575, 579
**self-contained
    problem,** 694
self-control, 485
self-critical, 696–697
self-deception, 168,
    170, 180, 351, 601,
    695
self-defense, 40, 235,
    404, 476, 532, 711,
    733, 753
self-destruction, 697
self-esteem, 171, 181,
    232, 342, 454
**self-evidence/
    self-evident,** 73,
    102–106, 109, 585,
    754
disbelievable
    self-evident
    proposition, 104
immediately, 105–106
paradigmatically
    self-evident
    proposition, 104
proposition, 104–105
withholdable
    self-evident
    proposition, 104
self-fulfillment, 173,
    696–697
self-hatred, 203
self-interest:
agent, 179, 183, 420
grounds, 139
Plato and, 129–130
rational pursuit of, 556
riches/wealth and, 129
**self-love (cf
    Eigenliebe,**

INDEX TO ETHICAL THEORY: AN ANTHOLOGY

Selbstliebe),
153–155, 195, 342,
493, 497–498, 503,
569, 670
self-moving, 310–311
self-preservation, 40,
503
self-punishment, 287,
290
self-realization, 204
self-regarding, 173
self-reliance, 657–659,
723
self-respect, 194–195,
587, 606, 742
self-sufficiency, 518,
618, 627, 657–658
selfitic/ unselfitic, 177
semantics, 29, 105,
573, 794
prototype, 790
sense of humor, 201
sense of self, 369, 574,
579, 658
senses:
evidence of the, 4, 55,
58, 76, 78
pleasures of the, 222,
268–270, 301
reliability, 76–78
sceptic of the, 96
sense organs, 75–77,
82
sense- experience, 761
visual, 81, 779
sentience:
adaptive characteristic,
384
behaviour of, 309
beneficiaries, 384
creation, 417
criterion, 387
draw up wagons
around, 385

epistemological
problems, 388
fetuses (non/sentient),
406–407
happiness, 659
human beings, 417
interest, 385–387
life principle, 387
limit of, 365, 384
moral consideration/
standing, 356,
384, 387–388
nonsentient, rights of,
580
physical objects, 668
pleasure/ pain,
300–301
potential, 384
sense experience, 356
suffering, 384
well-being, 64, 572
set:
amended, 578
coherent, 6, 119–120,
124–125
defined, 163, 719
determinate, 280
experiences, of, 85,
87–90, 92, 256
minimal, 726
ordered, 777
possible, 119, 577
rules, of, 227, 429,
451, 557, 611–612
standards, of, 163
sex segregation, 715
sex- announcing,
730–731, 734
sex-marking, 730–731,
734
sexism, 356, 362–364,
690–691, 729–731,
733–734
sexual abstinence,

379, 408
sexuality, 636, 641, 695
Shafer-Landau, Russ:
Ethics as Philosophy: A
Defense of Ethical
Nonnaturalism
(chapter 8), 54–62
Intro to Part 1 The
Status of Morality,
3–6
Intro to Part 2 Moral
Knowledge, 71–73
Intro to Part 3 Why Be
Moral?, 129–131
Intro to Part 4 Ethics
and Religion,
215–217
Intro to Part 5 Value,
255–257
Intro to Part 6 Moral
Responsibility,
305–307
Intro to Part 7 Moral
Standing, 355–358
Intro to Part 8
Consequentialism,
413–416
Intro to Part 9
Deontology,
481–484
Intro to Part 10
Contractarianism,
555–557
Intro to Part 11 Virtue
Ethics, 611–614
Intro to Part 12
Feminist Ethics,
689–691
Intro to Part 13 Prima
Facie Duties and
Particularism,
753–755
Moral Rationalism
(chapter 18),

70

159–166
Preface, xi–xii
Shakespeare, William:
King Lear, 294, 296
Merchant of Venice,
The, 721
Portia, 721
shame, 313, 327–328,
347, 742, 758
**shape (cf Form,
σχήμα):**
circle, 50, 626, 680
faces, 316
orthogonal, 777
overlapping, 777
triangle, 50, 760
Shaw, George Bernard,
201
Sher, George, 720
But I Could be Wrong
(chapter 11), 85–93
shoeless, 696
Shoemaker, Sydney,
157–158
should be done, 4,
138, 236, 437, 439,
455, 541
siamese twins, 393
side constraints,
482–521. *See also
constraint*
Sidgwick, Henry:
agent-based view, 660
Aristotle, on, 750
cases, difference
between, 788
casuistry, 785
common sense, 424,
750
consequentialism,
413, 452
equality, 428
Golden Rule, 528
imperatives, 24

individual actions, 423
Martineau, on, 659
Methods of Ethics
(1907), 298, 424,
457, 473, 534–535,
771, 785, 794
moral code, 469–470
principles behind rules,
677
prosecutor malice, 654
sinful cooperation, 524
universalizability, 27
unphilosophical
intuitionism, 787
utilitarianism, 363,
413, 424–425
utility (action vs
praise), 426
Simonides, 137
simple amenities, 533
simple ideas, 28
simple theories, 767
simpliciter, 152
sin:
alienation from God,
237
cooperation/
reciprocation, 524
desires/ passions, 559
original, 638
Singer, Marcus, 43,
525, 534
Singer, Peter, 63, 241,
356, 384, 389, 415,
482, 600
All Animals are Equal
(chapter 43),
361–371
Famine, Affluence and
Morality (chapter
53), 466–473
**Sinnott- Armstrong,
Walter,** 112, 125,
216–217, 735

God and Objective
Morality: A Debate
(chapter 25),
225–229
situationism, 776
skepticism/ skeptical:
Feminist Skepticism,
Authority, and
Transparency
(chapter 77,
Walker, Margaret
Urban), 735–750
general, 87
grounds for, 79, 94
knowledge of anything
at all, 71
moral, 72, 91, 94,
109, 455
problem, 327, 691,
736
radical, 71, 455
wholesale, 76, 79
worry, 72, 86, 691
sketch:
Alternative
Informed-Desire
Theory, of, 281–283
design, 181
good, of the, 618, 643
outline, 179
**Skinner, Burrhus
Frederic
(Skinnerian),** 464.
*See also Pavlov,
Ivan (Pavlovian)*
slave/ ry:
abolishing, 459, 462,
464
Caribbean (slavery),
461
citizens, 461
hereditary, 41
Juba and Camaica
(Cuba and

Jamaica), 461–462
nationalized, 464
owner/ ship, 41–42,
96, 459–460, 464
runaway slave, 228
society, 460
Sojourner Truth,
363–364
trade, 461
wage-slave, 459
What is Wrong with
Slavery (chapter
52, Hare, Richard),
458–465
Slote, Michael, 179,
190, 192, 613,
664–666, 675
Agent-Based Virtue
Ethics (chapter 69),
653–663
Smart, J. J. C., 210,
413, 456, 465, 720
Extreme and
Restricted
Utilitarianism
(chapter 49),
423–427
**Smith (fictitious
characters),** 58,
396, 576
Smith, Adam:
The Theory of Moral
Sentiments, 325
Smith, Holly, 789, 794
Smith, Michael, 6
Realism (chapter 9),
63–68
Smith, Robert, 371
Smith, Tara, 191
so forth, 789
social:
circle, 56, 454–455
contingencies, 678,
697

contract, 207,
555–557, 581,
591, 723
cooperation, 86, 154,
583, 588
entity, 146, 523
experience and
interpretation, 698
justice, 520, 583–585,
589, 591
maintaining social
order, 693
order, 20, 693
practices, 658, 691,
739, 747–748,
765, 777
presocial, 454–456,
578
science, 21
unrest, 123
utility, 350
social approval, 6, 45,
47
socialism, 227
**society (cf
Gesellschaft):**
Flat Earth Society, 96,
99
needs of, 469, 643,
657
pluralistic, 86
strange, 765
well-ordered, 583
sociology, 16, 21, 455
Socrates:
Euthyphro, 30, 215,
218–219, 228
Glaucon, 129
Immoralist's
Challenge, The
(chapter 15, Plato),
132–137
justice, 129, 572
virtuous people, 680

Sojourner Truth,
363–364
Sophie's Choice, 674
sophistical conclusion,
538
sophistry, 421, 536
Sophocles, 640
sorority, 722
**soundness (valid + all
premises true),**
58, 110, 149, 164,
243, 407, 787
South Sea Islanders,
493
special dignity, 139
special pleading, 463,
775
special science, 60
special sense, 141,
336, 472, 676
**species (cf Art,
especie):**. *See also
genus*
homo sapiens, 390,
393, 395, 397, 399
human, 14, 88, 356,
420, 665
our own, 13, 367,
369–370
threatened, 375
whole, 375, 699
speciesism, 356,
363–365, 368–371,
406
specious, 565
**spell/s (cf
Zauberspruch):**
beautiful maiden
under a, 377
spell-casters, 60
under the spell of
emphatic 'ought',
142

Spencer, Mr., 52
Spinoza, Baruch de, 656, 708
sport:
  animals, cruelty towards, as, 360
  desire for, lack of, 171
  luxury of, 193
  rewards (internal/external) of, 445
  World Series, 573
stability, 164, 381, 578–579, 588, 606
stable compliance, 579
Stalin, Joseph, 37
Stalingrad, 173
standard picture, 64–66, 691
standard view, 283, 645, 680
state:
  end, 523
  mind, of, 18, 53, 170–171, 185, 190, 256, 270–271, 294–295, 297, 301–302, 390–394, 398–399, 429, 442
  minimum, 533
  ultraminimal, 521–522
  universe, of the, 273, 299, 301
  world, of the, 327, 452
statement:
  ethical, 16–19, 28
  general, 175, 786
  ought, 24
statistical laws, 317, 781
status quo, 578, 582, 584, 612
steam locomotives, 580

steamboat company, 792
Steinbock, Bonnie, 406–407, 409
Stocker, Michael, 210, 722
Stoicism:. See also Stoicus
  desire, 290
  flourishing-based egoism, 192
  good, the, 292
  language, misuse of, 418
  liberty/ independence, 259
  megalopsuchia (μεγαλοψυχια), 635
  metaphors of health and strength, 656
  pain, 637
  Slote, Michael on, 192
  utilitarian principle, 258
  values, ranking of, 189
  virtue, 286, 635, 637
Stoicus, 268–270, 275
Stone, Christopher D., 389
story/ stories:
  competitor, 244
  crazy, 244
  deceive, intent to, 790–791
  fat man stuck, 537
  general perspective, 454
  Gyges of Lydia, 133
  happy ending, 243
  heaven and hell, 313–314
  infant development (Stoic), 641

Just So Stories (Rudyard Kipling), 60
Lazarus, 709
made up, 793
moral intuitions, mechanics of, 80–81
moral saint, 203
occurring to one, not another, 789
optimistic, 341
reading, 787
representation, 745
sophisticated hedonist, 445
Stoicus, 268, 275
Sullivan, Louis, 181
theoretical debate/ claims, 783
whole story, 706
Zeus, 633
straightforward maximizers, 576
stranger/s (humans, noun):
  act-utilitarianism, 433, 660
  commitments/ responsibilities, 745
  compassion for, 719
  death/ dying, 694
  foreigners, as, 284
  giving money to, 566
  good of, 191, 668
  lonely, 672
  obligations and, 718
  other-regarding, 153
  priority over, 186–187, 414
  proximate, 702, 710
  recovering/ cure, 294–295, 428–429
  sacrifices for, 433, 437

INDEX TO ETHICAL THEORY: AN ANTHOLOGY

Strawson, Galen, 305
Impossibility of Moral
Responsibility, The
(chapter 37),
312–316
Strawson, Peter,
306–307
Freedom and
Resentment
(chapter 41),
340–352
Streicher, Julius, 160
Strether, Lambert, 202
strict liability, 325
stringency, 112–113,
140, 154, 595, 763,
765, 768, 770
stringent duties, 768
strongly wanting, 298
subhuman, 41
**subjectivism/
subjective,** 17,
19–20, 23–24, 27,
29, 98–99, 429, 447,
594
inter- subjectivism, 24
moral, 23–24
reports, 23, 793
subjectivist, ordinary,
19
subjectivist, orthodox,
19
substantive:
basis of Golden Rule,
528
criterion, 383
difference, 530
distinctions, 382
good and, 49
historical allegiances,
777
interpretations of
impartiality, 788

issue of deserving
moral consideration
, 385
moral claim, 595, 598
moral issues, 328
moral requirements,
596
morality, 598
parallel, 323
questions, 378, 384
reasons to act, 120
restrictions on belief,
122
similarities (in common
humanity), 715
substantively
inadequate moral
theory, 739
truths, 108
Success Theorist/s,
295–297
sue for damages, 378
sui generis, 60
suicide:
duty not to commit,
503
ends and means, 496
experience machine,
264
FLO (Future Like Ours)
, 404–405
Kant on, 753
Logical Contradiction
Interpretation, 504
loneliness, 723
meaninglessness, 723
moral consideration,
388
natural actions, 504
Practical Contradiction
Interpretation, 508
rate, 536
self-love, 503
species, of our, 379

valuable future, 404
Sullivan, Louis,
181–182, 190
supererogation,
210–211, 415, 469,
533–534
superstition, 6, 115,
117, 171, 425–427,
597
supervenient, 29, 60,
787
supreme being,
231–232
surgery, 72, 95, 280
survival:
biological unsuitability,
379
feeling pain and, 366
harvests, between, 512
moral judgment, 698
morality, 225
right to, 375
self-caring, 695
self-serving device,
709
species, of the, 709
Survival Lottery, The
(chapter 54, Harris,
John), 474–478
survival qua man, 181
value, 87
wife's, 694
Swanton, Christine,
613
Virtue Ethical Account
of Right Action, A
(chapter 70),
664–675
sweat, 135
Sweden, 376
**Sykes, Bill (fictitious
character),** 97
syllogism/s, 401–402
enthymeme, 101, 781

hypothetical, 105
modus ponens, 60
modus tollens, 794
sympathy, 39–40, 56, 294, 326, 328, 340, 419, 446, 487–488, 494, 600, 713, 717, 763
syntax, 221
system of ends, 581, 585

T

tabula rasa, 677
Taj Mahal, 374
take account of, 525
taking a pill, 287
tant pis (cf. quel dommage), 477
tautology, 169, 174–176, 320–321
taxes for welfare, 584
taxonomy, 777
Taylor, Richard, 226, 240, 305
    Determinism and the Theory of Agency (chapter 36), 308–311
Taylor, Thomas, 361
technology, 46, 387, 389, 391, 640, 740
teenagers, 678, 680
teleology, 574–575
telling us what to do, 613, 676–677
temperament, 210, 324, 326, 328–329, 463, 487–488, 715
temperance, 622–623, 625–626, 667, 673
temperate, 622–625,

627–629, 665–667
ten commandments (decalogue), 247, 474, 478, 710, 757
tendency:
    agreement, coming to, 601
    bad conduct, 419
    causal relation, 759
    moral motivation, 600
    natural, 495, 626
    pain, shunning, 637
    promote valuable states of affairs, 670
    sentience, notion of, 385
    special, 494
test/s:
    causal test, 59–62
    holistic, 767
    phenomenological, 374
    Rawlsian test, 579
that-clause, 300
theism, 215–216, 223–229, 234, 236, 240, 242–245, 250–251
theology, 30, 222–223, 232, 252, 265
theoretical abstraction, 776
theory/ies:
    abstract, 436, 770
    anti-, 650–651, 738, 776–777
    cosmological, 574
    critical, 580
    decision, 125
    Desire- Fulfilment, 294–295, 428–429
    error, 26, 30, 79–82, 84
    ethical, 3, 7, 16, 22,

31, 35, 44, 48, 54, 63, 71, 74, 85, 94, 101–102, 106–107, 109, 112, 129, 132, 138, 144, 146, 156, 159, 167, 178–179, 181, 185, 193, 198, 200, 210, 215, 218, 220, 225, 230, 234, 242, 245, 255, 258, 264, 266, 271, 275–277, 286, 294, 299, 305, 308, 312, 317, 322, 330, 340, 355, 357, 359, 361, 372, 381, 390, 400, 413, 417, 423, 428, 441, 450, 458, 465–466, 474, 481, 485, 499, 510, 521, 524, 536, 543, 555, 558, 571, 581, 592–593, 611, 615, 630–631, 633, 645, 650, 653, 659, 663–664, 676–677, 689, 692, 699, 713, 721, 729, 735, 753–754, 756, 763, 772, 776, 785
    game, 454
    good, of, 794
    human action, 142
    implicit agreement, 40–41, 43
    impoverished, 689
    maximizing theory of rationality, 120,

126
metamoral, 210
Objective List, 296
over-simple, 323
physical, 34
practice, and, 447, 472
rational choice, 120
right action, of,
    677–681
rival, 597, 758
society, of, 591
Success, 295–297
theory can blind
    observation, 692
vague, 679
virtue, 630, 654, 675,
    777
    idiot savant,
        objections from
        the, 678
    loathsome advisor,
        objections from
        the, 678
virtue-ethical, 653
thinking clearly, 63,
723
thinking for ourselves,
682
third party, 475, 477,
661
Third World, 186, 510,
512, 514–515, 518
Thomas, Laurence, 722
Thompson, Janna, 666
Thomson, J. A. K., 675
**Thomson, Judith
Jarvis
(Thomsonian),** 84,
394, 399–401, 409,
483–484
    Killing, Letting Die,
        and the Trolley
        Problem (chapter
        61), 543–551

thought:
chain, 701
evaluations and, 185
experiment, 31, 240,
    256–257, 601,
    604–605
formal, 693
free, 641
freedom of, 586
fugitive, 141
logical, 692
moral, 5, 27, 29–30,
    216, 510–511,
    693, 717, 735,
    737, 746, 748–749,
    767, 786
one thought too many,
    206
operational, 693
private, 205
unreflective ethical,
    677
**Thrasymachus
(Θρασύμαχος),**
132–133, 137
threshold/s, 383, 430,
665, 667
tightrope walker,
184–187, 449
**Tim (fictitious
character),** 672
Timmons, Mark, 54,
112, 125, 685, 735,
784
to-be- doneness, 28,
601–602. *See also
not-to-be-
doneness*
told what to do, being,
678–679
toleration, 85, 669
Tolstoy, Leo:
Anna Karenina, 324

Tooley, Michael, 357
Abortion and
    Infanticide (chapter
    46), 390–399
tort, 376
torture:
accusations upon, 564
act utilitarianism, 415
baby/babies, 245,
    251, 773
blinded with fire, 134
children, 54, 73, 166,
    226
Control Thesis, 243
distress on hearing
    about, 279
five men vs one, 539,
    548
full information, 279
fun, for, 235, 251
God, 215, 245
hated rival, 89
infants, 251
innocents, 414–415
killing vs, 398
kittens, 678
moral absolutes, 226
moral rules, 415
permissible, 130
rule-consequentialism,
    437
sadist happy, making
    the, 754
saving from drowning
    to, 422
social rules, utility of,
    415
stretched on a rack,
    134
whim, 334
whipped, 134
wrongly despised
    person, 414–415
toti-resultant, 758

tout court, 669
tragedy, 294, 379, 404, 458, 709
trait/s, 54, 237, 611, 647, 670, 691
  character traits, 204, 206–207, 451, 652–653, 676, 785
transfer/s:
  belief, 531
  feeling, 699
  learning, 699
  rational- desire- transfers, 531
transformation, 265, 397, 643
transitional phases, 696
treating others as means/ ends, 108, 151–152, 206, 444, 496, 512–513, 515, 517, 519, 523, 606
trees:
  apples falling from, 60
  endangering, 375
  interests/ needs of, 386
  leaf/ leaves on the, 359, 389
  monkeys in, 793
  moral consideration, 375, 382
  oak tree, 135
  own sakes, 375
  parricide/ ingratitude, 13
  pohutukawa, 670
  redwood, 375, 377
  rose-bushes, 377
trickery, 40, 150, 484, 489
trolley cars, 580, 693
trolley problem, 79,

81, 84, 483–484, 543–545, 547, 549, 551
trust:
  arbitrator, 567
  beliefs, 115
  betraying a friend's, 188, 422
  bribery, 569
  collapse objection, 433
  common sense morality, 424
  cost of choices, 742
  covenant, 562, 564
  distrust, 51, 115, 143, 196, 455, 568, 701
  exceptions to rules, 433
  Hall of Holograms, 782
  histories of, 746
  infancy, 696
  internalized rules, 432
  intuitions, 74, 76, 82
  judgments, 638
  knowledge, 748
  others, from, 186
  promising, 503–504
  reason, 759
  saints (self-appointed), 448
  single individual, 666
  Trust and Antitrust (Baier, Annette, 1986), 720
  untrustworthy people, 684
  what to do, 741
trustees, 374, 376–377, 599
truth/s:
  a priori, 223
  analytic, 223
  conducive, 118
  falsehood and, 9, 64,

95
  minimal, 56
  necessary, 103, 221, 236, 239, 242, 245, 521, 586, 735
  real, 56
two hands, 94–95
Two Unique Cases of Preferability, 272

U

U.S.A. founding fathers/ revolution, 324, 363–364
ulterior motive, 142, 238, 658
unborn persons, 378
unbudgeability/ unbudgeable, 774
Uncle Fred (fictitious character), 779
uncodifiable ability, 682
underminable, 114
understanding (cf Verstehen):
  adequate, 104–105
  dispositional, 105
  mutual, 227
  obviousness vs, 101
  occurrent, 105
  principled, 693
  self-, 572
underwater, 695
unicorn, 175
unified system, 777
unifying enterprise, 108
universal (cf Allgemein):
  application, 476

generalization, 175
law, 206, 233, 239,
481, 488–489,
493–495, 497,
499–501, 503,
505, 507, 509
formula of universal
, 499–509
nature, of,
493–494, 499
medium, 210
**Universal Law,
Formula of,**
499–509
and universalizability,
500, 509
universalism, 526, 575,
663, 715
substitutionalist, 715
universality, 82, 443,
493–494, 497, 499,
501, 632, 661, 691,
696, 735, 737, 788
universalizability, 25,
27, 467, 481–482,
500, 502, 509, 534,
646, 689, 788
universifiability, 702
univocal, 149, 208, 656
untrustworthy people,
684
upper bound, 207
Urmson, James Opie,
423, 425, 469–470,
473
Utah, 376
utilitarianism:
act-, 414, 433, 660
calculation, utilitarian,
107, 204, 426
classical, 600, 649
conscience, 421
conscientious, 419

Contractualism and
Utilitarianism
(chapter 65,
Scanlon, T. M.),
593–608
extreme, 424–425
Extreme and
Restricted
Utilitarianism
(chapter 49, Smart,
J. J. C.), 423–427
hedonistic, 447
ideal, 757–758
normative, 596–597
one-eyed, 350
philosophical,
596–597, 600
restricted, 423–424,
427
rule-, 429–430, 660
Utilitarianism (chapter
48, MIll, John
Stuart), 417–422
utility:
actual, 125, 577
average, 603–606
considerations of, 421
doctrine of, 418
expected, 120, 125,
573, 591, 603–604
interpersonal, 125
interpersonal
comparisons of,
407
maximizing, 576
principle of, 120,
260–263, 420–421,
582, 611, 689
private, 418
requirements of, 419
social, 350

V

v-rules, 648–650, 652,
684
**validity (if premises
true, conclusion
true),** 746
objective, 19, 27, 30
value:
absolute, 458
expected, 456
instrumental,
255–256, 428
intrinsic, 30, 53, 166,
244, 250, 255–257,
272, 275–276,
413, 415, 447,
453, 456, 613, 755
justificatory, 117
loci of, 374
survival, 87
theory, 255, 413, 415
value theory:
philosophical, 255
pluralistic, 413
utilitarian, 415
values:
conflicting, 46
disvalues, 22–23, 778.
*See also system
of*
system of, 20, 210
van Gogh, Vincent, 255
variable (adjective):
action, parameters of,
693
inclinations or ideals,
534
intrinsic values, 276
moral obligations and
relativism, 145
variable (noun):
independent, 526

vegetable kingdom, 375

vegetarian, 91, 371, 636

vegetating, 377

veil of ignorance, 556, 581, 585, 587–590, 605–606, 714, 716, 725

Velleman, J. David, 280–281, 284–285

verbal:
definition, 49
discussion, 50
question, 48
questionnaire responses, 723
reports, 794

verifiability/ unverifiability, 4, 28

vicious people, 135, 273–274, 625

view/s:
external, 328
internal, 328
nonmoral, 123

villains, 546–548

violence:
coercion and, 512, 514, 517, 519
commonwealth (people) and, 566
destitution and, 513, 519
destructiveness of, 696, 698
dilemmas and, 697
gain and, 559
individual and group, 747
inequality and, 697
justification and, 749
kingdom of god and, 565

law observance and, 569
maxims of, 512
method, as a, 508
natural, 502
parasitic nature of, 508
personal, 459
physical, 527
renouncing, 357
to use others, 512, 518
unclear motives of, 561

violent revolution, 325

violinist, 401

virtual reality, 116

virtue/s, virtuous (cf Tugend):
active, 699–700
aim of a, 664, 667–668
Aristotelian non-relative, 630–644
Aristotelian virtuous agent, 665
being virtuous, 651–652, 676, 681–682, 685
development of, 681
ethic of, 700, 702
target of a, 667, 669–671
vice vs, 10, 12, 14–15, 25, 92, 136, 273, 275, 301, 569, 634, 649
Virtues Project, 676
virtues, the, 700
virtuous people, 157, 273, 435, 613–614, 627–628, 639, 648–649, 666, 673, 680–685

vivisection, 359, 416

Vlachos, Georges, 592

volition (cf Wollen):
analytic proposition, 491
conscious, 263
dissimilarity, 491
good in itself, 485
habitual, 263
imperative, 491–492
morally good, 489
motive, 495
objective ground, 495
original influence, 8
practical laws, 496
preventing, 8
reason, 8
world of ideas, 7

voluntary associations, 533

votaries, 572

vulnerable, the, 513–515, 690, 783

W

wage-slave, 459

Walker, Margaret Urban, 691
Feminist Skepticism, Authority, and Transparency (chapter 77), 735–750

Walker, Stephen, 371

want and desire, 491

wants:
conscious, 375
contingent, 527
disinterested, 527
immediate, 527
long-range, 527

war:
civil, 466, 559
just, 3, 404, 753

Warnock, Geoffrey J.:
beneficiaries/
maleficiaries, 387
moral relevance,
381–384
sentience, 385
warrant, 56, 75, 81, 93,
101, 107, 384, 449,
791–793
in argumentation, 77,
781, 789
Wason, P. C., 794
weakness of will
(ακρασία), 63
weighted amount, 522
weighted score, 522
welfare state, 518–519
welfarism, 284
well-dressed, 469
well-ordered soul, 153
well-roundedness,
201–202, 208
what comes from it,
132, 134
What else?, 790
what we (really) think,
152, 195, 302, 493,
618, 756, 758, 761
what we say, 375
whim:
desires, 288, 334
fathers as role models,
334
hitting a duck, 288
morality vs, 774
reasons vs, 774
tools, usage of, 522
whole race, 135
whole vs part, 117
whom should I believe,
691, 748
wicked/ ness:
Deity and, 238, 244
intention, 327

Ms. Goodwin (fictitious
character), 237
punishment, 216
successful, 565
v-rules, 652
wicked merchants, 537
widow, 376
Wielenberg, Erik, 217
God and Morality,
242–252
Wierenga, Edward, 244
Wilberforce, William,
96
will (cf Wille):
bad will (the), 322
determination of the,
326
free, 55–57, 59,
232–233, 265,
309, 312–313,
315, 317, 327,
330, 339
freedom of the, 315,
317, 319, 321,
326, 331, 339
good will, the, 322,
485
object of the, 231
weakness of (ακρασία)
, 63
will to survive, 457
Williams, Bernard:
alienation, 453
anti-utilitarian, 462
consequentialism, 450
conservatism, 453
Gauguin, 328
ground projects,
446–447
hope for truthfulness,
747
one thought too many,
206
responsibility, 452–453

sound deliberative
route, 160
subjective motivational
set, 160
transparency, 747
virtuous action, 631
Williams, Glanville, 542
Wilson, Cook, 301
Wilson, Timothy
DeCamp, 793–794
winner, 134, 243
wisdom (cf σοφία):
cowardice and, 185
God, of, 419
goodness and, 233
happiness and, 619,
627
nature, of, 486
path of, 414
power and, 216
practical, 107, 614,
632, 651, 665,
670–671, 674,
790, 792
result of, 185
summum bonum, 233
virtue and, 622
wit, 201, 485, 558, 565,
568
Wittgenstein, Ludwig
(Wittgensteinian):
antitheory, 738
codelike theory, 738
extra-theoretic, 779
language, 367
Moore and, 94
rule-guided, 779
Wohl, das, 300
Wolf, Susan, 330–339
Moral Saints (chapter
22), 200–212
Sanity and the
Metaphysics of
Responsibility

(chapter 40), 330–339

Wollstonecraft, Mary, 725

Vindication of the Rights of Woman (1792), 361, 689

work:
classic, 753
domestic, 690, 724
earlier, 439
good, 59
hard, 236, 275, 626
improved work conditions, 461
insignificant, 290
make things, 448
normative, 103
opting to work less hard, 430
original, 23–24, 29
real, 88
recent, 208, 611–612, 790
relief, 452, 511
short, 215
to eliminate slavery, 41
to work ill, 420

World Bank, 438, 466, 516

wrong (cf unrecht), 18–20, 37, 44–45, 220–222, 224, 427, 596, 702, 705–706
prima facie, 109, 765–766, 778
wrong-doing, 134

Y

Y and Z, 474–478

Φ

φ, 160–162

X

x-rays, 791

Printed in Great Britain
by Amazon